Louis,

Good luck w 71\1uu.

Best wishes

Ben Gaetos

I Dreamed,

I Ran,

I Conquered

A Filipino ultrarunner vs. Badwater 135 Miles

by

Ben Gaetos

First edition
ISBN-13: 978-1500714093

Edited by: Ivan Gerson
Technical Support: Paula Gaetos
Graphics Designer: Belle Hsu
Book design: Y42K Publishing Services
http://www.y42k.com/bookproduction.html

Table of Contents

Dedication

This book is dedicated to my late friend, Hervey who taught me that running is not just about hours, minutes and seconds. Thank you to my wife and daughter for keeping up with my passion for running, Mom for the prayers, family, A Runner's Circle, Team Ocho Crew, running and non-running friends for continuing to support, listen and read about my running journey.

Ben Gaetos

Prologue

Returning to childhood first love is like love the second and third time around. We separated and reconciled many times. Ultimately, we were meant for each other.

Don't get me wrong, I'm not talking about another woman. Running was my first love. This sport has accompanied me to tackle life's peaks and valleys, explore endless adventures, strive for racing glory, and dream improbable goals.

After finishing the 2002 Catalina Marathon in 4 hours and 21minutes, a runner from Chicago made a comment that my normal marathon times must be around 3:30s. He finished 4:45 and proudly owned a Chicago Marathon PR (Personal Record) of 3:40. We traded places in the early part of the race. Catalina Marathon was hilly while Chicago Marathon was fast and flat course. I replied that my recent marathon times were 4:15 at Los Angeles just two weeks before Catalina and 4:10 at Long Beach a few months prior. "How could you finish these races about the same time?" He asked. Running parallels with my life. It is a mountain full of peaks and valleys. When the going gets tough, the tough gets going. The way to defeat adversity is to try harder.

Running has led me to explore new heights and endless adventures. Every run is an adventure. I have made friends to people from all walks of life who shared the same passion. No adventure is small or big. From the very first step out of the doorway, an adventure is created. I've rescued lost pets and returned to their respective owners, found valuable items, gave driving directions, discovered hidden treasures of a town and many more. In one solo run, I passed by a familiar style of architecture. Building resembled work of the great master architect, Frank Lloyd Wright's textile block. It had to be. Eureka, I found it! I had no idea that Frank Lloyd Wright's La Miniatura Building aka Millard House is in Pasadena, CA near the Rose Bowl.

Grand Canyon, Kilauea Volcano and Mount Whitney are places normally seen on postcards or calendars. Running has set me afoot these picturesque places. Tourists pay hefty amount to fly over these destinations for a limited time. I get to see, feel, touch, smell and hear at close range almost at no cost.

"Have you won a race?" Almost all runners have been asked this question by non-runners. The truth is, just finishing a race is itself a victory. If anyone can run a marathon, then everyone would be doing it. Running brought me racing glory winning a few trophies, plaques and even first place overall. During the first eight years of racing, time was my primary goal. There were lots of pressure, injuries and personal issues which necessitated a break. Newfound interest in trails gave a new lease in life and peaceful mind. Competitive spirit remained but became secondary priority. One instance when a long time dream of sub-24 hours in a 100 mile was reachable, I took advantage of the opportunity. It may not happen again.

Finally, running has led me to dream improbable goals such as Badwater 135. In the beginning, I was just a spectator on the sidelines cheering for my heroes. The dreamer in me grew from a minute seed to a giant bean stalk. Then came my time to take center stage. Not too many people get a chance to fulfill a herculean dream. A chance to make history for my homeland, the Philippines was at stake. A friend said, "Show them what you're made of." I ran my heart out and kept fighting like I have always been in my life.

As I crossed the finish line, life is more than just a dream. I dreamed, I ran, and I conquered.

Ben Gaetos

Chapter 1: The News!

"Hello Ben!

Congratulations! You have been accepted to compete in the 2013 Badwater Ultramarathon, presented by Adventure CORPS, Inc. You are part of a select group who will participate in what is recognized across the globe as the world's toughest footrace."

"Shucks, what did I get myself into?" That was my immediate reaction when I received above email on March 7, 2013. I was extremely stoked and felt my heart about to explode. This can't be happening. Just minutes before, I received an email from Adventure CORPS, Inc. "Are you still interested in running Badwater Ultramarathon? We haven't heard from you." The invite letter was supposed to arrive three weeks prior. I threw out all hopes when notice wasn't received. However, I kept receiving Competitor Updates and was about to inquire. The race director insisted the invitation was sent on time. Maybe I received it as spam message. Just move on.

Unlike any other races, Badwater 135 Mile Ultramarathon is by invitation only where a five member committee selects 100 extreme endurance athletes in the world compete against each other and the elements of nature. Fifty veterans and fifty Badwater rookies comprised the field. This race is the holy grail of running. In 2011, cutoff time to complete the race was reduced from 60 hours to 48 hours making the selection more stringent. There is no prize money awarded to the winners. The much coveted belt buckle is awarded for those who finish the race within cutoff time. The men's course record is held by

Valmir Nunes of Brazil with a winning time of 22:51:29 set in 2007. Women's course record of 26:16:12 was set by Jaime Donaldson of Littleton, CO in 2010.

Fifty year old, Al Arnold from Pleasant Hill, California proved it possible in 1977. Arnold went solo. He didn't have any pacer to run alongside to share the suffering. His only support was a driver who kept dozing off in the vehicle. He ran and walked 145 miles from the lowest point in the United States in the town of Badwater, Death Valley, California 282 feet below sea level to the highest point in the contiguous United States at Mt. Whitney at 14,508 feet elevation. It took Arnold 84 hours to complete the feat. Third try was the charm as he failed in two previous attempts. Few others followed his footsteps until it became an official race. Years later, race was shortened to 135 miles up to Mt. Whitney Portal at 8360 feet elevation for safety reasons. Death Valley is the hottest place in the world. On July 10, 1913 Death Valley recorded 134F. 2013 is their 100th year anniversary. Race is held in July and covers three mountain ranges totaling 13,000 feet of cumulative vertical ascent and 4700 feet of cumulative descent.

Still shaken, I texted my wife and daughter for the electrifying news. Next to call, was Joe Matias of A Runner's Circle Running Shop. My friend, Joe had been pitching to sponsor the first Filipino to be invited to Badwater. His prayers were answered. A call to Nancy Shura-Dervin aka Ultramom followed. She is like mother to several runners including myself. For years, she has been trying to convince me to run Badwater. Retired Philippine Army Major General, Jovie Narcise received first hand news too. He opened the door for everyone to the sport of ultramarathon in the Philippines by directing the first Bataan Death March 102Km Ultramarathon in 2009. Text or email to close friends followed. "Which news do you want to hear first, the bad news or more bad news? The bad news is I got invited to Badwater. The other bad news is I have to run the race."

Most of the runners who were invited have already posted about their selection weeks ago on Facebook and other social media. I wanted to keep mine under low radar. Being on everyone's watch is not my cup of tea. My heartbeat remained upbeat until I got home. Only my daughter was home to talk about Badwater invite. "Yay, go Dad!" After walking our dogs, I visited my mom and told her the news. At 98 years of age, news like this should be carefully handled. She was excited and worried at the same time. Mom responded with, "You like putting yourself in difficult and dangerous situation. I always pray for you." My wife was finally home from work and I told her about Badwater. She replied, "Can you do it? You haven't run more than 100 miles and that's in Death Valley." I have to! This is history in the making as for the first time in 36 years, Philippines will be represented. There's a lot of stake and pride.

Forget about low radar. As soon as I logged in on Facebook late that evening, a couple of friends had announced that my name was in Badwater roster. Everyone eagerly waited for roster to be released. Congratulatory messages were so overwhelming. News spread like fire in the running community including Philippines. With the popularity of running soaring, the country's hope was on me. Talk about pressure, Badwater 135 is the beast among the beasts. Once again, David battles Goliath.

Call it "Sleepless in LA". Mind wandered the whole night. Most runners look forward to qualify or be picked in lottery at prestigious races such as Hardrock 100 Miles, Western States 100 Miles and Boston Marathon. In Badwater, it's beware what you wish for. Everyone supported and worried at the same time. I could die in this race. I've been to Badwater 135 twice as spectator in 2009 and crewed in 2010. A lot of lessons were learned from these experiences.

An opportunity knocked. I can't let my dream slip away.

Chapter 2: A Look back at the Past

Some runners were born to run. For others their dream was to run.

Born youngest of five boys and four girls, I grew up in a very dense community in Santa Ana, Manila, Philippines. One brother and a sister died before I was born. As a kid, I dreamed of being a jockey, news reporter, and track athlete. Learning ABCs and horse racing were learned simultaneously. My dad and eldest brother took me to the racetrack all the time. My other brothers and sisters tagged me along on musical events and movies. Running interest came from watching Olympics television coverage. Childhood games included racing in the street when free from evening traffic. Running interest drew little as basketball remained primary sport until today. Other sport gets recognition only if an athlete wins a world title or performed exceptionally well in international event.

Dad worked as a delivery truck driver for Mountain Province bus, Dangwa TranCo in Manila. Mom was housewife and a seamstress. Her claim of fame was making dresses for famous movie actress and across the street neighbor, Rita Gomez in the 60s. Due to limited resources, education was strongly emphasized in the family. It was the only way to better living. We didn't even own a television set. After homework, I watched Combat on Friday nights and Saturday morning cartoons from our neighbors' window. It took years until we owned a television. My eldest sister, Tessa shipped a Philco TV from the USA. Tessa worked as nurse in Canada and the USA, studied to be anesthetist and retired as administrator for a major hospital. She was main breadwinner of the family. Two of my brothers earned full academic college scholarships. They also assisted in family needs. As youngest sibling, I was lucky to be sent to Catholic school. Rest of the siblings studied at public school. Mom also adopted two of her younger brother's siblings.

Heart failure at age 60 caused the demise of my father. Every weekend, fellow drivers rested from a long drive and brought exotic foods for drinking session at our house. They made me sample their foods. Dad's sister was prominent in Baguio City, Mountain Province. Grandma lived there and was never close to me. I don't remember her showing me affection until she passed away. In contrast, I was favorite grandchild of my other grandma. She peeled cacao seeds for me all the time and lived 100 years. All rest in peace. Dad passed away when I was fourteen. He only bought me two toys, a jeep made of recycled tin cans and a used three wheeled bicycle which I kept for long.

It was difficult growing up. My older brothers looked after me. Mom opened up a clothing store in nearby public market. I tended the store and if sales were good, earned extra money. Living in a rough neighborhood, I held my own and hustled money at the pool table or wagered in any improvised street games with kids some of whom became notorious gang leader, goons and drug dealers. And yes, there were fistfights too. Our street was battleground of rival gangs. The sounds of homemade shotgun, sling fired makeshift arrows and drunken individuals were normal. Taxi drivers feared and wouldn't even take passengers to our street.

Collegiate days at Dominican Order, University of Santo Tomas in Manila paid little attention to running. There were other sports but I didn't have the height or physique. My first choice in college was psychology but job demand was almost nil. Second choice, Engineering demanded lots of work. High school adviser recommended Accounting. Nope. Architecture sounded interesting and had short admission line.

A plateful of partying, rock concerts and violent fraternity activities got into the mix. College was complete freedom compared to hard lined high school. Oftentimes, my system was loaded with substance and battled cold sweats during sleep. Anxiety drugs, stimulants, cough syrups, pot, experimental highs and alcohol proliferated in school and neighborhood. My cabinet was full of vinyl records which were frequently borrowed for parties. Some landed at second hand shops to purchase concert tickets. After concerts, there were close calls eluding military curfew hours during late President Marcos regime. There were anti-government protests during martial law. It was too violent and some were orchestrated by subversive people. There were too many acts going around. Call me "the quiet storm", close lipped; I knew sources of drugs in and out of the campus, horse racing, jai-alai and illegal gambling activities. In spite of my association with the dark side, exemplary education from Paco Catholic School earned me Bachelor of Science degree in Architecture in 1979. I often skipped classes and still topped test scores in major subjects to the envy of many.

The teachings at PCS were far advanced. I may have gone

astray a few times but my upbringing directed back to the right path. In 2008, a class reunion was held in Las Vegas, NV attended by USA and Canadian residents. It was the first time for many to meet the opposite sex. Boys and girls occupied separate campuses. Everyone was proud of their alma mater.

Living in the material world, my family was not. My parents gave me the best gift in life; that was a quality education.

Chapter 3: Reality Test

Move over Ozzie, Benny had his own reality show before you.

After college, I immediately found a job as civil engineering drafter at Metropolitan Waterworks and Sewerage System (MWSS). It was a huge office handled by American consulting firm, Camp Dresser and McKee, International. There were several work disciplines such as architecture, structural, civil, electrical, and mechanical engineering. Mom didn't have to worry about me. She migrated to the USA a week before my first day of work. Her visa sponsored by my sister, Tessa was finally approved. MWSS salary was better and more stable than other small offices I applied. Thus, I was able to assist financial needs of the family. There was no need to ask my brother for allowance anymore. Maturity hit me. My brother also entrusted me to design his house and oversee construction.

Things went well at work, freed myself from substance abuse and were on fourth year of a relationship with a girlfriend. After eight gainful months, a series of setbacks fell like domino to include abrupt end of a relationship, blew one month's salary in horse racing in one weekend, alcoholism, and worst of all failed my architect license test. I did not study diligently but there was no way I failed Structural Design part unless test scores were switched. In fact, I aced it. My academic grades in Mathematics and Structural Design throughout college were always 2.5 to 1.5 (85% to 94%). In the Philippines, grade of 1.0 is the highest. Academic grade of 2.0 (86%) and above exempts a student for finals. Results were tainted with suspicions. Several test candidates were out of the examination room way too early and in the waiting area smoking in relaxed mood. I was talked into a payoff beforehand. Doing so would taint my family's reputation. My brother topped his Mining Engineer license test. His school gave him a victory parade for being Number One. I was completely crushed and sorry for disappointing family's expectations. Life hit bottom.

Down but not out, I vowed revenge and focused on my career seriously. Most of my close friends at work had left to work in Middle East countries. Work contract was usually 1-2 years but paid triple compared to Philippines salary. I could have joined if I wanted to with their recommendations to their employers. I didn't follow suit as my application to migrate to the United States was already on file. A fresh start was needed to get back on track. Transfer opportunity to field office opened up. I wasted no time. There were too much drama and gossips at the main office which I didn't want any part. Results of previous architect test came under protest but no change in outcome. New board of examiners weeded the undesirables.

Working environment at construction site was more conducive and educational. The project was a huge pumping station and reservoir. Meanwhile, I religiously prepared for the test and was busy on outside work involving architectural design and drafting. All roads led to positive direction. Gambling came to halt after a streak of winnings at horse racing. Better to quit when ahead. It was also at the field office where I met my beautiful wife, Josephine for the second time.

She was receptionist at the main office but never said hi to each other. We became good friends. Our married boss had an eye on her. Close relationship developed, dinner and next morning we asked each other, "Are we dating?" Relationship went under everyone's radar until an observant engineer aka "The Godfather" noticed. Godfather and I worked moonlight. When news broke, the boss summoned me into closed door man to man conference. Boss was mad. Josephine left the office to work in their family jewelry business. New receptionist was hired. This time, no personal conversations were allowed at the office. Receptionist desk was moved inside the conference room with view window to the office. It took 2-3 months before everything went back to normal.

Soon the much awaited results of the architect license were published on newspapers. Short list included my name. Only 167 out of 347 successfully passed. Last time, more than 1000 candidates took the test. I raised my hands in joy and pointed to the Man above. Redemption fulfilled and whole family was proud including Josephine. Respect was earned. For the first time, one well off relative called me "Cousin". I couldn't believe it. We really were first degree cousins as one of our parents were brothers and sisters. Teenagers in the neighborhood sought my advice on everything and were everyone's "uncle." When working late nights on projects at home, teenagers listened to music below my window. On my break, I came down to have a shot of their drinks. I didn't mind as long as they keep the noise down. It was also a lot safer to avoid getting busted.

Let bygones be bygones. The boss needed professional

expertise in architecture outside work including his apartment. He and I undertook architectural and structural engineering design for a major commercial savings bank. He was the front man. Our electrical and mechanical staff engineers were assigned some work too. I stayed late after work for those projects. When done, a utility driver gave me a ride home.

Life was good. Halleluiah!

Chapter 4: Off to the U.S.A.

Uncle Sam, here I come.

It was only a matter of time that the long awaited visa to immigrate to the United States came to fruition. Mom applied for my petition as single individual. My visa was approved in 1984. I had to leave Josephine in June and came back a year after to marry her. The downside was that my immigrant status couldn't bring her in the US automatically. It took six years before my wife and daughter followed. In between those years, the only resort was visiting Philippines frequently like overseas workers.

Not too many professionals landed with the same profession in the United States. Out of nine resumes mailed, one of two offices responded for interview. I stayed briefly with my sister, Tessa until I found a job. She took me to a high school track near her house where she walked and played tennis. Running was infused to my vein again. In August, Ziegler, Kirven, Parrish Architects in Los Angeles offered me an entry level architectural drafter position. Thanks to my alma mater, University of Santo Tomas. ZKPA had great results from UST graduates. Back to square one. I needed to start somewhere.

I moved to the house of mom's eldest brother, Uncle Ben when I found a job for easier commute. He took me to nearby Echo Park where he walked daily. Work became hectic that running was set aside. Living in the US, it was work, work and more work for long hours. Once settled, I rented an apartment and took care of mom. She worked as seamstress in

LA Downtown Garment District. Mom's friend at work was married to an architect, Tibor Kiraly. He needed some part time help. After ZKPA hours, I went home, grabbed a quick bite and worked 3-4 more hours at my second job. Earnings were definitely good but very stressful unlike Philippines.

Running came to the picture again late 1986 after I worked full time to the architectural office of Kiraly and Associates. He and his wife were of Hungarian descents. The office was busy but without militaresque environment like ZKPA. Tibor's projects were mostly single family residences, apartment buildings, mini-malls and carwash facilities. ZKPA's projects were school facilities, military facilities, utility facilities and medium sized commercial plazas. Both offices gave me lots of experiences in the types of construction in the United States.

Obtaining architect license in the US was not my priority. My priority was to be together with my wife and daughter. I considered one time not to return to the US and stayed in Manila for almost seven months. A teaching opportunity at my college alma mater was offered by my former class adviser, Architect Simoun Soriano. Philippine economy was not going any better. Thus, I returned back to the US. I met new contacts in contractors, interior designers and metal louver manufacturer. I worked as independent contractor and shared office with Tibor and a couple of architects. There was no such thing as paid holidays for independent contractors. You're on your own in terms of employment benefits. Even weekends were working days.

More work meant more income. In 1989, I saved enough

money for down payment to my own condominium. It was a long search for the right house for the right money. There were close purchases but patiently waited for the right one. The property was two-bedroom townhouse in Eagle Rock part of Los Angeles. Environment was good and still close to several services and work commute. There were a lot of cheaper houses but daily commute was not convenient.

Running activity continued for mere twenty minutes about twice a week. I eyed for my first race, Run for the Homeless 10k at Griffith Park in 1989. The course was my training ground. Finish time was 51 minutes and 26 seconds. The late Los Angeles Mayor, Tom Bradley fired the ceremonial starting gun. Running briefly with the lovely Olympic track and field champion, Florence Griffith-Joyner prior to her unexpected demise was awe inspiring. She was very humble person. A month later, I signed up for another race to improve my time.

US economy hit recession. Tough times loomed. Work suffered slow down too as our major clients suffered losses and moved out of California. I started to worry as my family was soon to have their visa interview. As independent contractor, I don't have extended family benefits. Medical and dental coverage costs were sky high. When Josephine and Paula finally arrived, we finally spent our time together. In November 1991, I was hired as civil engineering drafting technician by the City of Los Angeles – Department of Public Works. Starting salary was lower than previous earnings as independent contractor. However, health coverage such as medical and dental was included. Employee vacation and sick leave were also included. To offset income loss, I picked up small jobs in drafting architectural plans. I came to the US as an architect, ate my pride to work an entry level position. Why not, challenge myself to push for my architect license? That would be great too.

The hills of life are always alive with challenges. How thirsty we are for a particular goal, is up to us. I asked myself. "Do I fold or do I stay." I stayed.

Chapter 5: Rollercoaster

The thrill of victory comes with agony of defeat.

Competitiveness soared to higher level when first ever trophy was earned at a 5k race, Crippled Children's Guild on February 12, 1995 at Griffith Park. I didn't learn of my triumph at the finish. Notice arrived the day after that order of finish was reversed as two runners were disqualified for cutting the course. I leap frogged to third overall finisher. Trophy and prizes followed.

As proud as it can be, trophy symbolizes success in any endeavor. A few top three age group wins followed. Family members and friends began expecting for more. As I developed more of a runner, pressure started building up. There were invites from running shoe companies to join their team. Sponsors demand a lot from athletes even as part time. Full time job and family would be difficult to balance should invitation be accepted. At that point, time was already being juggled at several activities.

Intensive training led to injuries such as plantar fasciitis, sciatica and lower back pains due to overtraining. Without proper coaching, sources of information were limited to books and running magazines. Running clubs were only a handful and tailored for fast competitive runners. Running friends either moved or quit running. Thus, there was nobody to relate with. Marathon best or PR (Personal Record) of 3:47:00 in 1996 nosedived to 4:25:00 in three years. Depression followed along with somewhat frustrating professional career direction. State of California does not recognize foreign architect license outright. Therefore, I had to pass architect license in California for better promotional opportunities. The set of written tests was a big hump after being away from school for a long time. Once a licensee candidate successfully pass the written portion, the candidate then go through oral interview from a panel of examiners. Both professional career and running zeal headed south. I was in my low point again. If I could salvage one more win, I can hang up my running shoes in high note then carry the momentum into my professional license. Nope.

North Hollywood High School Bulldog 5k in June 1999 was the perfect race. Victorious in previous year's age group, a repeat was very much doable. To my disbelief, race was so disorganized. Major street intersections were unmanned causing runners to cut course. Throw away sub 20 minute PR. Finish times were unresolved and no winners were declared. Phone calls and letters to the race organizers and school fell on deaf ears.

Idle for five months, life was so different. I met Jon who was then boyfriend of my wife's best friend, Minh. Jon used to run in his collegiate days and had been running sparingly. We signed up for a 5k run. I gasped for breath almost the entire way and finished miserably in 28 minutes. Jon and I became friends and signed up for more races.

Meeting pet and poultry supply store owner, Hervey re-ignited my running interest in January 2000. His physical condition at sexagenarian age was amazing. My primary goal was to complete ten LA Marathon finish. Hervey talked me into running Catalina Marathon scheduled two weeks after

LA. Catalina Island is 25 miles from Long Beach. All hotels were booked but found a camp site available. Remarkably, I finished in 4:59:38 which many said was close to a sub 4 hour marathon on flat roads. Catalina Marathon course was dirt mountain trail. The experience introduced me to trail running. The following year, I came back and recorded a faster 4:21:16. Hervey, Jon and I ran races together even in pouring rain and muddy conditions. A new chapter of my running career was born.

In order to get back to competitive form, I joined Club 26.2. Training runs were held at Marina Del Rey. Under Coach Mills, I was able to finish Portland Marathon in sub- 4 hours (3:56:17) in 2001. After a year, I left the group and stepped to ultramarathons.

New found interest in ultramarathon came about during a training run at Griffith Park. Jimmy whom I met at Catalina Marathon introduced me to a tall skinny guy named Flaco (Spanish for skinny) and a bulky Carlos both from Mexico. Carlos stated they already run 80+ miles the past weekend. No way. I thought he was talking trash. A month later, I found out that Flaco finished an impressive second overall at Angeles Crest 100 Mile Endurance Run. I met a few runners including top gun, Jorge Pacheco. Introduction to coach of Ultraladies and Men Running Club, Nancy Shura led me to my first ultramarathon finish at Bulldog 50k in 2002.

Professional career had its own struggles. I gave up on taking the architect license exams. Memory retention had drastically diminished unlike younger days. A lot of my college peers didn't pursue higher aspirations. They were intimidated and worried what people would say in case of failure. Others gave up trying and settled as drafting technicians. After some deep soul searching, I stood up, fought back and successfully passed my State of California Architect license.

Dreams are made to be chased. They are always ahead of us. You cannot rely simply on hope and prayer. You don't pass if you don't study. You don't finish if you don't train. The same goes in life or in races.

I Dreamed, I Ran, I Conquered

Chapter 6: My first Marathon

On you march. Get set. Go! This command wakes my senses all the time. I had always imagined myself running track when I was a kid.

The 1991 Los Angeles Marathon was an eye catching race. Mark Plaatjes of South Africa won the race with a tactical move. Mark grabbed the lead at Mile 6 at Sunset Blvd. past Chinatown and never looked back. His close competitors and television commentators thought he would fade. No sir, Mark was only coasting and had plenty of gas left to ward off challengers. That race started it all and dreamt someday I will complete a marathon too.

Far from the leaders, my former co-worker at MWSS, Joe ran the same race in 5-1/2 hours. We used to drink all day and night. If he could do it, I could too. That was sufficient motivation for me to run 26.2 miles. Joe used to me a member of a running club in the Philippines. Mine was All Star drinking club. Back then, running clubs in Los Angeles were mostly for fast runners. Talk about training partner, my mom used to join me. She walked on Sunday afternoons with me while I ran for an hour at Griffith Park or at the Rose Bowl.

March 1, 1992 arrived and there I was afoot the start of Los Angeles Marathon in front of the historic Los Angeles Memorial Coliseum. Joe did not run but offered me a ride to and from the race. His late night work shift at Home Depot and family obligations conflicted with his training runs. My longest training run was probably 16 miles. Theoretically, a marathon training program lasts 26 weeks. I had no program to follow. Just run!

Nervousness was gone as soon as the music of Randy Newman's, I love LA was played. Ali, Ali, Ali chanted the crowd while the retired boxing champ waved his hands to about 15,000 runners. Running through streets of Los Angeles was a huge block party. Surprisingly, there were cheaters on the race. Several runners hid behind bushes and waited for the main pack then joined. It took me almost five minutes from my starting position to the start sign. Those cheaters only fooled themselves. Being at the back pack early meant holding my pee. The very first parking lot at the race became automatic restrooms for male and female runners. Nobody cared.

Church bells were rung. Weddings during the race and variety of entertainment featuring cultural dance, live bands, cheer leaders and taiko drummers energized the runners. Young kids extended their hands for hand slaps and high fives. Spectators also handed out water, oranges, and candies aside from the water stops and electrolyte drinks. These were repeated in every mile. I have never been in such as huge event like the LA Marathon. Excitement was in the air.

Reaching virgin territory around Mile 18, my feet began to hurt from blisters. As a rookie, I did not pay attention of my beat up only pair of running shoes and cotton socks. I had only one pair of shoes, a Nike Pegasus. The worn up sole was even patched up. Race started at 9:00 am. Near noon time, it was hot. Cold water sponges handed by cheering crowds along Hollywood Blvd. at Chinese Mann Theater were a life saver. "You can do it. You can do it", they yelled with their bells or noise makers. I ran in spite of the pain.

As runners turned to Crenshaw Boulevard and Jefferson Park, a procession of runners limped. I never knew the term "wall" that Joe mentioned. I literally thought we would scale a fence wall. My legs began to cramp and heavy about Mile 20. Some residents sprayed water hoses as well as fire trucks. Cheers from crowd helped me dug into my second, third or fourth wind. Limping in pain, excitement increased when I saw Mile 24. I jogged slowly until I found a rhythm. As the crowd noise peaked decibel reading, the Coliseum appeared in sight. I was there during the 1984 Olympics and saw women's marathon finish inside the Coliseum. I imagined the same too. My childhood dream was happening. It did!

The timing clock flashed 4:09:52 at the finish line. It never stopped. The beginning of an epic journey had just begun.

Race Reports

Races and adventures are always exciting moments. Racing is not just about who has the fastest time. It's a reunion of friends and meeting new friends all with a common goal of crossing the finish line. Whether a runner is competing for top honors or just the joy of finishing, every runner has a story to tell.

The following races and adventures are worth remembering. Their paths led me to Badwater 135.

Ben Gaetos

Chapter 7: My First Ultramarathon - Bulldog 50k Trail Run

Malibu Creek State Park, Malibu, CA
September 7, 2002

The saying goes, "First won't be the last." I have always been mystified by ultramarathon. On race day, I felt more nervous as veterans talked about past and future races. Secluding in my car was far better than socializing.

As the race started, I picked up a quiet spot. Fellow newbies from Ultraladies and Men Running Club, Sue and Red called my attention from far end of the line. They reminded me to follow Coach Nancy's advice to start slow and run a smart race. My goal was 6- 1/2 hours finish. I even taped a cheat sheet showing locations of steep hills.

The first few miles were relatively easy. We passed through ruins of the vehicles used in the TV hit series, MASH. The long steep climb at Bulldog Trail followed. We have trained on this section numerously. Magnificent ocean views and San Fernando Valley can be seen 360 degrees. I picked up my strides after reaching the peak. So far, so good was my progress.

Gravity took over as rocky trail descended to Tapia Park. It was a Catalina Marathon déjà vu as I passed several runners leaving Sue and Red behind. An aid station was set up at bottom of the trail around Mile 17. After refueling, a stream crossing at Tapia Creek made the race interesting. A 30k option was also offered for less adventurous runners. The 50k

41

and 30k runners split ways after crossing knee deep water. Chart indicated another uphill climb from Mile 17-23. Mercury started to boil at this point. I was not present when our group trained for this next segment. Sporting squeaky wet shoes, I began my climb to this snake like rugged single trails. I was alone and hoping I was on the right trail. Sue, Red and I got lost in one of our training runs. Voices from beyond began to close in as I caught up with a few runners. Faster runners were also coming down opposite direction. One runner yelled, "The turn is few yards away". You're right!! I heard that a while back. Finally, an honest sign indicated "Aid Station and turnaround 2 miles away".

In marathons, volunteers hand a cup of water to runners at aid stations. Here, volunteers assisted runners like NASCAR pit tops. Volunteers knew exactly what you need such as filling up water bottles. Foods offered variety of choices from peanut butter sandwich, bananas, oranges, M&M, cookies, etc. You don't need a food critique to know which food was best. After refueling and refreshing with ice cold water sponge, I was now ready for downhill run.

Downhill single trail switch backs, needed a lot of eye and foot coordination. I was moving fairly well. Soon enough, I felt my legs heavy. I downed an energy gel and electrolyte pills to prevent leg cramps. I was now on virgin territory beyond 26.2 miles. The last aid station Mile 28 was within reach. Upon reaching the aid station, I took extra time to refuel. There was one final climb before leveling to the finish. A volunteer gave me encouraging parting words as I left the aid station.

Bulldog 50k did not have loud cheers and glamorous

finish like marathons but my heartbeat reached high decibels. Coach Nancy welcomed me with open arms. Finish time indicated 6:21:40. I called up my wife and my friend, Hervey to share victorious moment.

Mission accomplished and this was just the beginning.

Ben Gaetos

Chapter 8: San Diego 100 Mile Endurance Run

Lake Morena, CA
October 21-22, 2006

Like first love, SD100 was hard to forget. My arrival to the 100 mile world was so memorable that I had to run four extra miles to earn my buckle.

Race day atmosphere was like a marketplace before dawn. Caffeine was definitely on everyone's vein except mine. Mt. Disappointment 50k race director, Gary Hilliard asked if I have a crew. He quickly offered his services when I said none.

As the sun rose, the picturesque surroundings awakened my senses. Fall colors, undulating desert and mountain views, Salton Sea, and rock boulders deserved a second and third look. Location, location, location as real estate agents would say. My pace was two hours ahead of 29 hour goal and felt great. Realistically, that feeling was temporary.

Halfway at Mile 50 Banner Store Aid Station, darkness painted the scene. Injured runners dropped. Nervous runners panicked for flashlight batteries. Gary summoned me like a boxer while I was downing a cup of noodle soup. "Sit down. Look, listen to me. Slow down. You're way ahead of schedule. This is not a 10k race. I want you to finish. You have all night to finish even by walking. Slow down. Understand?"

Shortly, the role of a pacer struck my mind. It was still a long way to have my pacer join me at Mile 76. Meanwhile, the strategy was to keep in visual contact with other runners as much as possible and followed ribbons for direction. I was in virgin territory beyond 50 miles. Race commemorated my late father's birthday. His spirits kept pace.

Upon reaching Todd's Cabin Aid Station - Mile 76, my pacer and good friend Jon waited inside a warm cabin. Outside temperature started to drop. Jon had no pacing experience but I was more comfortable running with a close friend. Gary already left home but gave instructions. Time was about 3:30am. Race tempo shifted from power walk to snail pace as we hit rocky trails of Pacific Crest Trail. PCT stretches from Mexico to Canada.

Sunlight finally arrived at Fred Canyon Aid Station - Mile 89. Easy to think there were eleven miles left. Tired legs thought otherwise even with Jon's encouraging. Second wind was missing or maybe snatched by the Santa Ana winds. After checking out at the last aid station, Boulder Oaks six more miles remain. Think 10k. Jon offered to buy coffee if we finish before 11 am. "Sorry Jon, make it beer instead. You know I don't drink coffee." Slowly, I picked up the pace and in running mode. Think beer, think beer.

With about two miles left, an unexpected twist marred the race. A botanical researcher innocently tagged vegetations with same pink colored ribbon as the race. I noticed two ribbons at a trail split. Wait a minute, something must be wrong. Finish line should be somewhere near. I saw the researcher and inquired directions to the finish line to Lake Morena. "What race?" he replied. We were lost and traced back the route. A few runners followed the wrong direction until we traced PCT Trail.

"Did you really run 100 miles?" my wife asked when I crossed the finish line. "You looked like you've just run a marathon." I did...only it was four times.

Chapter 9: Death Valley Trail Marathon

Death Valley, CA
February 3, 2008

"Yaa Whoo! Titus Canyon Road is open." This was the race director's last minute email the day before the race. What's in this marathon anyway that runners all over the world would flock for? Hotel reservations were fully booked and expensive that we stayed in less visited distant town of Beatty, NV. I'll soon find out why the race sold out fast. The plan sounded exciting for my family too.

At 7:15 am, about 300 runners assembled at Furnace Creek Ranch for race briefing. Runners were then bussed to the start at Titus Canyon in Beatty, NV. It was a clever idea to cover two states in one race. Race description stated that course ascends 2,300 feet in the first twelve miles and descends 5,000 feet over the last fourteen miles. Aid stations are five miles apart. Daytime temperature is in the 60's. An alternate course along the highway was planned in the event of heavy snow. Around 1 pm on Friday, US Forest Service declared the trails safe to run. This was a rare occasion.

The first few miles of Titus Canyon Road were on a gravel jeep road. My goal was just to finish under five hours. The only attraction thus far was the distant snow capped Sierra Nevada Mountains and gigantic Mount Whitney. A few sections of the road had snow berm shoulders. Some runners were deceived by the flat appearance of the road and sped up. I was satisfied with my pace not knowing what to expect.

At Mile 10, it was time to pick up the pace. The course started to become more interesting with winding short up and down fire roads. Near the bottom, I was suddenly awed by the spectacular view of the Red Pass Summit up ahead at 5250 feet. This was the beginning of a number of eye popping sceneries to follow. The dirt road transformed into red with snow patches of about two inches. A number of runners stopped to take photos of the poster like scenery. Wait a minute, these people must be tourists disguised as runners including myself.

At the summit, I switched to high gear. Thanks for the fourteen miles of mostly downhill. The trails turned into gravel again as it connected back to Titus Canyon Road. A looming view of the upcoming gigantic rock boulders made me slow down. As I entered the boulders, I heard approaching footsteps behind. There was no one behind. After a few stop and go, I felt spooky then realized the footsteps were actually an echo. Who said hallucinations only happen in 100 mile races?

Just after Mile 20 aid station, the boulders would soon be behind the runners. Wide open view of the desert sand dunes were in sight. Trail conditions were back to ankle twisting loose gravel roads. I was more careful this time as I hit ground in the first few miles. My pace was still in high gear and continued to pass runners. Volunteers at Mile 23 aid station informed that finish line was about a little more than four miles. A marathon is 26.2 miles. With added distance, this race was actually an ultramarathon by definition. I stepped one more notch to finish in high spirits at 4:42:11.

Some races are meant for racing against time. Death Valley Marathon is not designed for this purpose. My wife, daughter, our dog May-may and running buddy Hervey completed a wonderful weekend. Yaa Whoo!

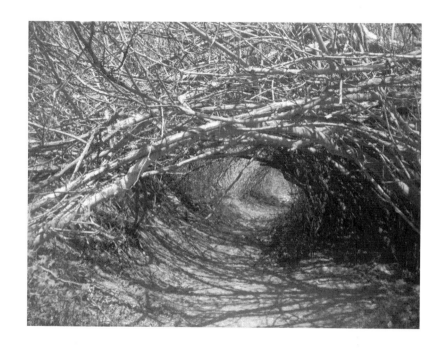

Chapter 10: Old Goats 50 Mile Trail Race

Cleveland National Forest, CA
March 28, 2009

Promises are made to be broken. It may be true in politics but not in ultramarathon. Race director, Steve Harvey kept his promise that the Goat ranks among the toughest fifty milers in the country.

Runners were bunched up in single file during early miles. It was rocky and rolling single trail track with an early morning chill. The first aid station at Mile 6.9 caught my attention immediately. One volunteer packed the aid station on horseback. They served doughnuts and my favorite breakfast, pancake. Why in the world did I choose ultramarathon as a sport anyway? My friend, Carmela yelled at me, "Dude, remember you signed up for a race and not IHOP. Let's go." She was referring to the restaurant, International House of Pancakes.

Quickly the twenty one mile loop was gone. We were back to Blue Jay Campground for our cars as extra aid station. My eyes popped as I stared at a mountain peak that leads to the next aid station at Mile 24. Simply said, Main Divide is Holy Jim's little brother. As Steve stated, there is 12,000 feet of climbing in this race with a continuous 4000 feet climb from Holy Jim Canyon to summit of Santiago Peak.

The sun's heat intensified as climb progressed. There was no shade at all at the fire road. A sudden boost of energy built up when I saw two mountain bikers pushed their bikes uphill. As runners approached Mile 24, Led Zeppelin's "Heartbreaker" was being played. Volunteers informed me that the next five miles is steep, rocky single trail downhill. Super, let's rock and roll!

Swiftly, I gained ground on runners navigating the trail of loose rocks and thorny bushes that defines the Trabuco Trail. I trained a lot on similar conditions. As the saying goes, what goes down must come up. The dreaded 7.5 mile climb up Holy Jim Canyon to Santiago Peak was awaiting its prey.

After hydrating, I power walked another technical single trail. Several hikers wore big smiles descending the trail. They probably thought we didn't realize what was ahead. There were stream crossings and tunnel like arched bushes. After climbing five miles, Bear Spring Aid Station Mile 34.1 greeted runners with hot noodle soup, quesadilla and other foods. My SoCal friends manned the station with a personal touch. In addition to Steve's statement, the aid station ranked among the best. After refueling, it was onward to another three miles of climbing to Santiago Peak summit. Words of encouragement posted along the trail were exceptional with the last one being, "Your prayers will be answered." Soon enough angels complete with wings and halos greeted runners with their needs. One angel was even playing harp.

After Santiago Peak Summit at Mile 37, the major climbs were over. Only a few minor ones totaling 1500 feet in the last thirteen miles were left. Regardless, the finish line was still far away. Darkness loomed with rolling fire roads and I had my flashlight ready. The lights of Lake Elsinore were in a distant view as well as the surrounding valley. Watching sunset without a drink was uncharacteristic. Cheers anyway.

As the finish line approached, my question on why I chose ultramarathon as sport gave me the same response again. It's a priceless feeling to taste this sweet victory. The time 13:31:00 didn't reflect slow or fast times. The finisher's medal said it all. We're proud to be one baaaaad Old Goat.

Ben Gaetos

Chapter 11: Mt. Disappointment 50 Mile Trail Run

Mt. Wilson, CA
August 8, 2009

"When is your next race", asked my co-worker the day before my 3-day weekend?

I replied, "This Saturday if my ankle heals on time".

A week before this race I turned my ankle while warming up for Aztlan 5k Trail Run at Elysian Park which resulted to a DNS (Did Not Start). You read it right, a 5k Run – the perfect training for a little speed work. A test run on Friday revealed unpleasant results. My running friends concurred that running a 50 miler would be inadvisable.

On race morning, I carpooled with a couple of runners to pick up my race packet. The least I can do was to support my running buddies. Fifteen minutes before the start, legendary Eric Clifton was in barefoot. I asked him if he had switched to barefoot running. He softly responded that he forgot to pack his shoes. "No way, are you serious?" I asked what size he wears. 10 ½, he replied. "I'm 10 ½ and not running, why don't you try mine," I said. Just try to keep it clean.

During the race, I drove at aid stations to cheer runners. I took pictures and rang Xmas bells. Unlike marathons where mega crowds cheer, ultramarathon is as serene as it can be. Aid stations are oasis in mountains. A sudden boost of energy pumped up whenever their names were called. One volunteer from Foothill Flyers Running Club greeted runners half mile

Ben Gaetos

to the top of the hill of Shortcut Saddle Aid Station. Runners couldn't figure how the volunteer knew their first names. They were unaware that he had a copy of the entrants list. Shortcut AS Mile 41 is a crucial part of the race. It's a continuous seven miles of exposed uphill fire road. This section has always been an ugly scene. In 2007, several runners including myself nauseated at 105 degree weather. The Search and Rescue Team man this section carefully. This year the running gods gave us a favorable weather. Immediately after the last runner left Shortcut, I proceeded to Mt. Wilson finish the second time.

Atmosphere was very festive and merry at the finish. Runners were welcomed with big cheers. Men's 50k winner went to unheralded Thomas Crawford of Monrovia. Local favorite, Jorge Pacheco finished a close second. In the women's 50k division, Michelle Barton won uncontested. First place in the Men's 50 Mile division went to Guillermo Medina from Santa Maria. A surprised, Diana Treister snatched the 50 Mile women's division. She had tears of joy as her hard work paid off.

Meanwhile a few runners were still navigating their way at the final 5.3 mile signature climb of Mt D. Kenyon Devore Trail has steep single track rocky switchbacks. Even a non-believer would seek divine assistance on this infamous climb. Darkness loomed as the cutoff time of 9:30 pm approached. Crowd began to dwindle as only families and friends of the remaining runners patiently waited. News of struggling runners was also relayed. The biggest cheer erupted as last finisher, Vinnie Torres tearfully arrived.

As I drove back with my buddies, we talked about their epic battle. I honestly considered running at the last minute if I didn't run into Eric Clifton. But what if I injured myself more? I definitely will attack sections of the trail that I could run. Unprepared runners betting their chances on hopes and prayers are the first one to tumble.

True, I DNS but my shoes did the running for me. Eric Clifton shared his 1st place age group and top 10 overall with me. I just hope he'd share some of his mojo too.

Ben Gaetos

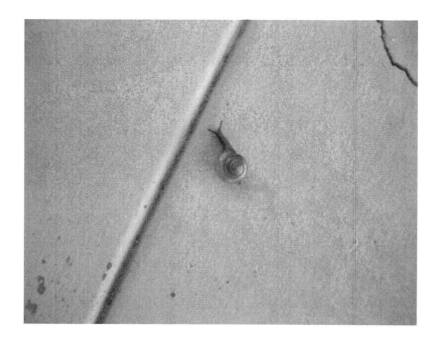

Chapter 12: Spooner's Cove 50k Trail Run

Montana de Oro State Park, CA
Nov. 20, 2010

"You're in first place and actually winning the race", said volunteer friend, Catra as I completed my first loop. Surprised! Yes, of course.

Rain forecast scared off potential runners as rain poured all night. One must be certified crazy to even think of running in wet conditions. I am probably one of those in races such as Chimera, Catalina and LA Marathon. Most runners safely opted for 25k or less. Runners I met on race day felt sorry for me to run two loops. What others didn't know was that I'll be enjoying the gorgeous scenery twice as Mother Nature granted perfect race weather.

The first three miles were along winding dirt trail along the bluff with views of the rugged cliffs and sandy beaches of Spooner's Cove. Flock of sea gulls stayed atop rocks to view giant waves in musical fashion. The pack of runners was still intact and in jovial mood. Thereafter, it was time for serious running as the course proceeded to short mild climb and downhill single trail. A sweeping turn led runners to face the beast, Valencia Peak.

Runners quietly navigated magnificent 360 degree view of the coast and the Morro Rock landmark. The course then continued downhill through layered rocks and tall overgrown bushes heading to the staging area at Mile 7.

The second beast awaited us. This time, Hazard Peak was more of a haven for mountain bikers. It was not as punishing as Valencia Peak but nevertheless a serious climb. I passed a couple of runners and maintained within reach with another for directions. I can't be too anxious as I need energy for the second loop. My elapsed time for 25k showed 3:18:--. Thereafter, the real excitement began to unfold.

The Race Director and Catra informed me that only two runners showed up for the 50k. I felt embarrassed and thrilled. No question, it was still an official race. Last time I've been this close was a 3rd place overall finish in a 5k fun run in 1994. This was an opportunity of a lifetime. I didn't want it to slip away. Thus, I prepared myself for a battle. No more taking pictures as I felt being hunted by a predator.

Midway of the climb, I looked back to check my competition. Someone was moving at a steady pace along giant bushes about 200 yards away. Without hesitation, I set my strategy to get to Valencia Peak asap. If I can get to the summit first with a good margin, I can pull a victory. My downhill skill will take care of the rest. As I turned around the summit, there were no visible individuals other than hikers I passed. Smell of victory was in hand. As I reached the staging area now Mile 23, I was informed that the other runner DNF'd. All I had to do was to finish in one piece. Again, I felt embarrassed but who knew that Mother Nature would play major part in the race. My friend, Hervey and I braved 3.5 hours of driving from Los Angeles at 3 a.m. on race day under scattered rain. A division place for Hervey in his division was also very rewarding experience.

Snails win races too.

Ben Gaetos

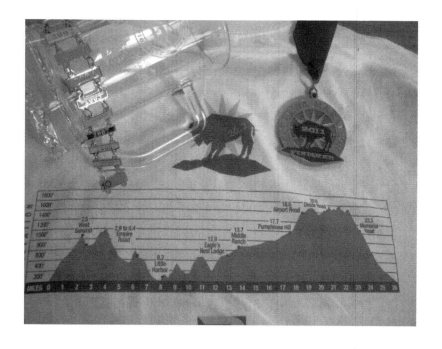

Chapter 13: 34th Catalina Marathon

Catalina Island, CA
March 12, 2011

"It's the greatest cult race", described *Runner's World* magazine. True to its billing, the turnout was exceptional albeit tidal wave warning caused by Japan's tsunami. Travel remained under precautionary conditions.

The marathon started at the other end of the island, Two Harbors which was another 45 minute boat ride from the main town of Avalon. The course traversed mostly hilly dirt fire roads through the island's less traveled interior and finished in Avalon. This race is not for speed seeking marathon PR runners. Isaac Newton's Law of Gravity mathematically applies here, what goes up must come down.

At the out start, frontrunners and backpackers etched the steep profile of the course. I took a short and easy stride knowing that there were plenty more to come. Every turn during the first couple of miles gave runners a glimpse of magnificent view of Two Harbors. More gorgeous views were expected ahead. It was just a matter of how fast or slow one gets there. This is probably the primary reason why runners keep coming back to this race.

After 2.5 miles of climbing, the course roller coasted to the island's interior. The gorgeous flora and fauna was well preserved under the Catalina Island Conservancy. I was tempted to push the pace in the downhill sections but payback loomed at the more challenging second half. Still, I was comfortably passing runners until we reached sea level again at Little Harbor.

The remotely located Little Harbor is ideal for camping and other activities. The scenery was overwhelming making runners stay longer break at the aid station. It's packed with foods, hydration needs and even a shot of spirited drink. A payphone served as a lifeline for anyone contemplating of dropping out. Sorry to say, the only way back was to face the daunted hills ahead.

Around Mile 12 - Eagle's Nest Road, the course gradually climbed endlessly through the historic Eagle's Nest farmhouse, stables, and nursery gardens. My Garmin GPS indicated 2:23:-- at halfway mark. My previous time was a disappointing shade under five hours. It's still respectable but par below my normal finish. I've run all but one since 2001. Last year, schedule conflicted with my mom's 95th birthday celebration. Best days are over but quest for time pumped my adrenaline.

My snail pace was still steady at the deceivingly flat Middle Ranch Road. I jockeyed position with other runners confident of reeling them back at the top of Pumphouse Hill and Airport Road around Mile 19. A reward of a well stocked cheerful aid station waited at this dreaded climb.

A couple of short hills lined up as the course pass trough mountain ridge. Avalon was in sight down below with refreshing breeze well timed for the finishing kick. Another look at my Garmin projected a time under 4:45:--. "My wheels are good, enough gas in the tank and downhill just around the corner, let's do it," I uttered. The last four miles of downhill has always been my best friend as I passed runners within sight. I was in a position to break 4:40:00 again with a mile left but losing ground. Thanks to the crowd near the finish line, I clocked at 4:39:27.

People leave their heart in San Francisco. I left mine at Catalina Island.

Ben Gaetos

Chapter 14: 26th Los Angeles Marathon

Stadium to the Sea
March 20, 2011

It never rains in Southern California. Runners who wagered on this saying lost big time as heavy storm and winds hampered the 26th edition of the LA Marathon. I didn't plan to run this year. However, the sudden demise of my friend, Hervey made me run in his honor.

Runners welcomed the course change in the first three miles to include Chinatown and Little Tokyo. Sounds of Japanese taiko drums pulled me to the top of the hill at the Music Center. I wore a poncho over a windbreaker right after the start as slight drizzle dropped. Brave ones wore a simple shirt and a few had no shirt at all. Not a smart move.

My goal was to finish around five hours after having completed hilly Catalina Marathon the previous week and a tough Old Goats 50 miler scheduled following week. There was no need to push for time. The plan worked in the early going. Approaching Echo Park Lake at Mile 6, heavy rain poured. Quickly, I changed my plan to speed up as dark clouds covered the city. My hat's off to the Angeleno crowd who once again showed 110% support.

I always loved running through Sunset and Hollywood Blvd. It's the most scenic in my point of view as well as an exhibit of various cultural ethnicities. On a clear day, runners face the panoramic view of historic Hollywood sign and Griffith Park Observatory. Iconic buildings such as Hollyhock

House, Chinese Mann, Kodak, and Pantages Theaters lined up along Hollywood Blvd. An array of cultural diversities too was present such as Hispanics, Thais, Filipinos, Jewish community, etc.

By midway, rains stopped briefly from West Hollywood to Beverly Hills. Spectators were kind enough to offer oranges, strawberry, banana, candies, cookies, Vaseline, Gatorade, coconut water and energy bars from 99c store. The overwhelming hospitality of the crowd made LA Marathon world class event. The course had been revised numerous times in response to religious, political and business reasons. Even runners have their own complaints too regarding hills and weather. The bottom line was that you can't satisfy everyone. Phideppides delivered messages on foot regardless of conditions. Just do it!

Around Mile 18 at Century City, aka "the wall", the lively atmosphere changed. The downpour had been on and off. A number of runners labored on the side of the road not only from cramping but also hypothermia. An inexpensive poncho or a trash bag can make a difference to protect the body from the rain. Even with a poncho and a windbreaker, my entire body was soaked. Yet, some runners thought they can beat Mother Nature's fury. Paramedic trucks became a common sighting. Thanks to these people as well as the energetic volunteers who braved the weather conditions handing water and Gatorade at every mile even on flooded streets.

By the time you know it, the race entered the homestretch at Westwood / West LA. The cheers grew louder as the crowd encouraged runners that finish was near. I was still moving at a constant 10 min/mile pace and reeled runners one step at a time. The last three miles was a fast downhill leading to Ocean Blvd. at Santa Monica. Mother Nature unleashed its heaviest downpour entering the last mile. Hervey would have loved this extreme condition. Together with his spirit, we finished in 4:27:23.

This one's for you, Mr. Chapman. Thank you.

Chapter 15: Leona Divide 50 Mile Trail Run

Lake Hughes, CA
April 30, 2011

Today's Special: Scenic Pacific Crest Trail with a mixture of fire roads spiced up with gusty cold winds and relentless climbs. This is just a perfect weekend menu for the palate of trail hungry runners. What more, they have 13 hours to feast. Let's check it out.

For appetizer, the course started with cardiac test of 3.5 miles uphill from Lake Hughes Community Center. Weather forecast of gusty winds was accurately predicted as it hit the canyons early. I wisely paced with my running buddies, Carmela, Donn and ultranewbie Kimberly instead of battling the weather gods. Soon enough, we had a breather of calm winds until we reached PCT at Mile 12.9 Aid Station. The pace picked up albeit packed on gorgeous single trail downhill with wildflower accents until Mile 16.4 Aid Station.

From here on, main dish was served. I went first as my running buddies lagged behind. Having run the old course, my mind was calmly set to climb seven miles to the turnaround. Changes were made last year in which I DNS (Did Not Start). The new course climbed 10.6 miles followed by 2.5 miles downhill then back the same way. No wonder there were no leaders in sight. When they did, it was very dangerous to yield at narrow trails. The stop and go motion threw my rhythm off until the course opened up to a fire road.

Just deal with it!

The presence of ultra-maestro, George V with his unofficial aid station at the fire road was magical sign of relief. He reminded me to make sure to eat at the turnaround Mile 29.5 Aid Station. Most runners were crawling back at this long climb and it's about noon. I ate half of my subwich plus protein drink. From thereon, my rally began as I cheered other runners in the opposite direction. I also thanked George for his inside information upon my return.

The downhill fun began as I shifted to auto pilot gear. The magnificent view of surrounding valley and undulating mountains was much clearer in the later part of the day. I gained step by step on runners ahead. As I inched closer to one runner, I noticed her strange gait. I asked if she was okay. She responded that she had blisters and asked if I have blister tape. I normally carry a first aid pack and gave her one. The next aid station was about two more miles. Thereafter, I continued my onslaught until the bottom of the course at Mile 42.6.

There were lots of people cheering at the aid station comprised of family members and friends of runners. The main courses were served. Now, it's time for dessert. I had plenty of room for that. A couple of my friends, Anibal and Carlos assisted me with food and drinks to fuel the last four miles of ascent. I grabbed a cookie, Coke, Gatorade and an organic drink from Anibal. On the way up, I passed tiring runners until I reached Mile 46.1 Aid Station. After exchanging pleasantries with volunteers, it was time to finish off my plate.

It took me 11:14:01 to finish a bountiful feast of trail

running. Mark your calendar for another Leona Divide festivity in 2012. I can't wait.

Ben Gaetos

Chapter 16: Bishop High Sierra 100k Ultramarathon

Bishop, CA
May 21, 2011

Amidst doomsday prediction, small flock of runners took their chances at this year's Bishop High Sierra Ultramarathon. A gamut of races was put together by race director, Marie Boyd. Before it's over, I'd like to take a peek at paradise.

The first six miles were rolling sandy dirt road with panoramic view of surrounding valley and picturesque snow peaked mountains. My heart beat faster at every step gasping for precious air. Everyone turned into silent mode as altitude increased. That wasn't for long as aid stations were strategically placed. Lo and behold, Buttermilk Road Aid Station served hot blueberry pancakes. I wasn't competing for first place. An extra minute for pancakes won't hurt. Buttermilk AS at Mile 11.27 marked the turnaround for 20 mile runners. The 50k, 50m and 100k runners continued thereon.

Scenery changed as course passed boulder formations, tree vegetations, wildflowers and the constant view of snowy mountains. It wasn't as hot or cold unlike previous years. How could weather be this good on Judgment Day? More uphill remain as course approached Edison Loop Aid Station Mile 17.40. Runners passed this station three times. The road leading to Edison Loop was very rough and rocky. I stopped on a creek crossing planning my move. Luckily, a runner coming down pointed a safe detour. I was comfortably ahead on cutoff time. Thus far, my lungs handled the 8000 feet altitude well. I'd soon find out as I was three more miles away to Overlook Peak at 9400 feet. Keep hydrating, I kept telling myself even early in the race. Approaching the peak, a foot of snow covered sections of the road. Never mind the missing snow man, Overlook Peak was the most spectacular part of the race. Eureka! It was paradise at Mile 20.39. Again, another extra minute of stay won't hurt.

Coming down Edison Loop #2, I filled my stomach with solid food from my backpack. We're still in high altitude and upcoming trails were rugged rolling hills. The section leading to Bishop Creek Lodge turnaround was unending path. I dug deep within myself even as the race wasn't halfway yet. Unbelievable, it was only Mile 29. This time, I left the station quickly. There was nothing wrong with the foods or volunteers. In fact, the race was well supported. I was just eager to make up time. When I reached Intake Aid Station the second time, I was 1:45:00 ahead of cutoff which gave me a very good cushion. Downhill sections ahead would work to my advantage.

Moving along, I reached Edison Loop #3. This time, it was now Mile 35 and warm. I had full confidence of finishing. Previous finishers told me final 12 miles were difficult both mentally and physically. Thus, I took a few walking breaks even on the descent. I had to slow down as the uneven rocky road was difficult on my quads. I passed a few exhausted runners who voiced to downgrade to 50 miles. They gave me well wishes.

Unfortunately, I was misdirected to the 50 mile finish by the timer when I checked in at the last aid station. Campers along the course cheered for my finish to my surprise. I knew there were a few miles left. My GPS indicated close to 50 miles upon nearing the finish line banner. The race director greeted and handed me a medal. Did I complete 50 miles or 100 kilometers? Immediately, I notified the race director of the mistake.

A few runners told me that I should be upset. I'm just happy; the world is not over yet. I'm still alive and had a chance to take a peek at paradise.

Chapter 17: Angeles Crest 100 Mile Endurance Run

Wrightwood, CA to Altadena, CA
July 23-24, 2011

"Forgive me Father for I have sinned. I swore not to run AC100 again. Yet for the 4th time, I couldn't resist temptation."

Wrightwood (Mile 0) to Islip Saddle (Mile 25.91) went conservative as planned. Thereby, I observed the natural beauty and surroundings of Angeles National Forest more including sunrise. Being calm meant no gasping for air climbing Acorn Trail and fear of Mt. Baden Powell towering 9400 feet. Weather forecasted scorching temperature. Yet, some runners hammered the downhill early. One must be patient to defeat this beast. AC100 pays no mercy.

Heat intensified after Islip Saddle. I didn't lose weight at first mandatory medical check. The chicken rice soup that my crew prepared was welcoming present. I focused on Chilao Aid Station Mile 52.80. I kept drinking iced water, coconut water, Saltstick, protein drink and solid bites. The trails at Cooper Canyon exhausted me despite conservative pace. I sat down for the first time at Cloudburst AS M37.54. Two of my veteran ultra friends, Cheryl and Jakob gave me encouraging words. Chief crew, Rebe handed a protein drink. My friend Carmela's husband, Gus as always offered a hand. I planned to pad time at the next five miles of downhill. To my despair, legs had nothing and were relegated to walk. A few runners

81

passed without challenge. Total despair continued until Chilao. My projected 30 hour pace diminished to 32-33 hours cutoff. My goal was 31 hours or better.

DNF (Did Not Finish) went through my mind at Chilao. My weight was up by 1.5 lbs. mostly from negative thoughts. I sat down with weary legs and mind. My pacer whom I talked to the night before was a no show. While eating and hydrating, I noticed that two faster runners were in deeper hole. I asked my crew, Rebe for second serving of beef tri tip. Cheryl, who just completed Badwater Ultramarathon at 120 degree temps, assured me temperature will drop soon. At 8 pm, mercury was still boiling. I touched my bib with my sister's name written. She is fighting cancer. I told myself, "We will overcome this together".

Lo and behold, my second wind arrived as I passed several runners going to Shortcut Saddle M59.30. Gus uttered, "Dude, you gained time." I was pumped up to see more friends. Going down the fire road leading to Newcomb AS, I felt blister on both heels caused by running down on loose rocks. I should have tightened my laces hours ago but kept postponing. Puking zone must have moved early as there were several spots leading to the stream. My level of confidence skyrocketed but wary of letdown. Just don't be too confident. Headlamp started fading but enough to read the trails.

At Chantry Flats M74.55, I regained my weight. My second pacer, Jay was present. I changed socks, shoes, replaced batteries, ate and greeted my friends. I also asked for updates of my running friends. AC100 vets say race begins at

Chantry. No one can save a troubled runner after Chantry. There is no crew access until the finish line.

Jay did most of the talking climbing 5.5 miles to Mt. Wilson Toll Road. Soon, he'll step up to the 100's. City of Pasadena below was painted with colors of second sunrise. This fueled energy to my system. Downhill followed and then endless uphill inferno to Sam Merrill while avoiding poison oaks and toxic poodle bushes. The sign at Sam Merrill M89.25 said, "It's all downhill from here". They should have added, "And it's rocky". My blisters grunted running over rocks. I just dealt with it and continued passing runners in the final stretch.

Coming home it was an enormous welcome. 71 out of 123 starters finished. Buckle #4 was most difficult but achieved fastest in 31:41:12. AC100 showed a sneak preview of heaven and hell. For penance, just let it be in miles.

Ben Gaetos

Chapter 18: 31st Avalon 50 Mile Benefit Run

Catalina Island, CA
January 14, 2012

One down and 49 miles to go. Time was only 5am but lots of energy was in the air as a record registration of 320+ runners formed a sea of lights on moonlit mountain trail. My goal was to start my 2012 races in upbeat note. Last year was my worst finish in five tries at 10:48:00. A wake up call is needed.

Watching sunrise at Catalina Island is an element of beauty with picturesque scene of clouds battling which color would prevail. Avalon 50 is not to be underestimated to begin with. The altitude is less compared to most races. However, the long steady slope punishes every runner equally.

I ran together with my two friends, Drew and Kam early while exchanging training tips for Angeles Crest 100 Miles in July. We have lined up several preparatory races leading to the big dance. Drew and I also trained together in preparation for Avalon.

The race didn't really begin until Mile 18.7 at Little Harbor 1. The support was commendable except for sliced raw potatoes at Mile 6. Our trio ran and power walked comfortably. Give credit to the overcast weather unlike last year's unusually hot day. The next 7.8 miles to Two Harbors can make or break a runner's dream. The magnificent views around the island kept us going. The leaders led by eventual champ, Fabrice Hardel worked their way back to the finish.

85

Kam slipped a few strides back but was moving well. Runners as early as 10 pm Friday night led by 80 yo, Hal Winton was also on his way back. Runners who can not meet the cutoff time were allowed an early start. That was fair deal.

The first half of the race went through as planned a shade less than five hours. The big climbs were stacked hereon. Temperature was still within comfort range approaching noon time and early afternoon. Drew and I were a stone throw away until Little Harbor 2 at Mile 35. He spent a few minutes longer. I walked slowly and waited until I decided to proceed. We'll meet at the finish.

I kept within pace and switched places with other runners. Middle Ranch section of the course is what we call the dullest area. The road looked flat but actually a long gradual uphill. If I can reach Pump House at Mile 44 with enough fuel in my tank, I can blast the last four miles of asphalt downhill. Thus, I power loaded with energy drink, pretzels and boiled potatoes at Pump House. It's time to go. I need to catch my boat back to the mainland.

Turning to the downhill homestretch, my senses were further awakened by a screaming truck passenger. She yelled, "Run baby run" while flashing her tops to a few of us. "Am I in Hollywood Blvd.?" You know, sometimes it's good to be slow. I floored the gas pedal to 7:30s per mile passing several runners at will.

"49 down and one mile to go", signaled my GPS watch. The first of 2012 races planned was off to a good start in 10:10:25. One race down, more races to follow.

Chapter 19: 2nd Bataan Death March 160k Ultramarathon

Mariveles, Bataan to Capaz, Tarlac
Jan. 28-29, 2012

1 mile = 1.6 kilometers (km), Deg C to Deg F. Who would know running in foreign soil requires crash course in Chemistry? Don't forget, no calculators allowed.

I ran BDM 102k in 2010. FYI, that's about 64 miles. A family vacation coincided with BDM. Question is, am I ready? BDM is the brainchild of retired Philippine Army Major General Jovenal Narcise to commemorate fallen WWII - US and Philippines soldiers.

74 runners navigated the first seven kilometers of narrow zigzag uphill road in darkness to meet their support crew. My goal was to finish in 26 hours. If the stars lined up properly, I'll push for my lifetime goal of sub 24 hours. Divine assistance is readily accessible at each town's churches. My crew was once again led by my nephews, Albert and Balong, cousin Jun and his son, Richardson. The addition of BDM finisher, Dess's expertise would be an ace factor. Other friends I met at BDM102 were either running same race or crewing another runner. Game on!

The first 35km of rolling pavement suited my running appetite. Overcast temps favored the runners early followed by rain and heat. Humidity remained constant equation. My crew kept me cool every three kilometers by spraying water, ice cold towel, and ice cold water bottle. The sudden change in weather worried concerned residents. "Where is your start and finish? You can get sick running that far."

The two-lane highway flattened after 35km. Rice fields kept the area green. Along the roads were various food chains and fresh coconut and fruit vendors. Say no to headphones. You'll learn to recognize the size of vehicles by their sound from the big trucks to the king of the road, tricycles (motorcycle cabs). Always be ready to jump to the shoulders.

Splits at Km 80 (50 miles), was just over 10 hours. Dess questioned, "Are you going somewhere? Are you in a rush? You're passing runners one by one." At Km 102 checkpoint, I was surprised to learn about my 5th overall position. The crew lost me briefly due to darkness. Dess and Albert had to run me down. It was time for my mandatory food break of porridge with boiled egg. First time ever my stomach had zero violent reaction.

Several obstacles developed during the night. Pedestrians and glare from vehicular traffic scattered everywhere. There were no more kilometer marker monuments to follow. Distance became a guessing game. I had to change shoes back to original which was soaked from the rain. The replacement didn't have enough cushions. A deep pain underneath the ball of my right foot developed. Every attempt on running was uncomfortable. I can't bend for proper gait. Thus, power walk was the only option. Move!

Another BDM finisher, Jerry paced me on the spot. Angeles City was like Las Vegas Strip weaving through traffic. During the presence of US bases, live bands proliferated. Today, it is the videoke (video karaoke) bars.

Kilometer or miles didn't matter anymore as I stopped my mental calculations. So close but yet so far. The town of Capaz was all I wanted. It is the gateway to the historic BDM Shrine. Pain remained plus new blisters. Dess switched pacing duties entering Capaz. Sub 24 dream was still within reach if the winding uphill road would only end. Time slipped away at the turnaround. I looked at the stars formation. At the same time Dess voice out, "we'll get sub 24 even if it's a second left." We sprinted and finished in 23:57:25 placing 8th overall.

It's not a dream anymore.

Chapter 20: Coyote 2 Moon 100 Miles

Ojai, CA
March 9-11, 2012

Can a group of runners of different speeds run together for 100 miles? Call it a long shot. The "8 Team" was up to the challenge.

After two years of cancellation due to severe weather, eight ultra buddies sought the elusive C2M buckle on its last year of existence. Captained by lone lady, Coco Pimp, the group vowed redemption with Castaway, Jumpin' J, Leap Frog, Buckle Hoarder, Ultraholic and Happy Meal. Newbie, BenWah Balz was suckered into the fray. The group set aside PRs (personal records) and agreed to run together. Total elevation gain and loss for C2M is 28,000 feet which is more than Angeles Crest and Western States 100 Miles.

The 4:00 pm start guaranteed two nights of full moon mystiques. Happy Meal opted for 100k beforehand was late but caught up. The Team navigated the early hills in festive mood. Pace was neither slow nor fast. Jumpin' J radioed the tandem crew of Linda and Gus before arrival to Sisar and Thacher School Aid Stations. Unlike other 100 milers C2M aid stations are 10+ miles apart. It's like a mother sending off kids to school with packed lunch every time they left aid stations. C2M couldn't be more eventful without the celebration of Ultraholic's birthday at Thacher. No candles but bonfire and singing happy birthday greeted the celebrant.

For most part, fire road was brightened by the full moon.

Flashlights were optional. The priceless feeling of being close to nature is hard to explain to a non-runner. Thirty-five miles into the race, the Team began to tire at Cozy Dell Aid Station. The group rested longer than usual. Almost everyone spent time taping their feet. Ultraholic took a nap inside the car. Surprisingly, Jumpin' J wore knee support. Oh no! He knew the trails blindfolded. Castaway and BenWah still led but the rest couldn't keep up with target pace to Gridley Top.

The Team reached Gridley Top just before sundown. There was no food to eat but coffee was offered by aid station captain, Mauricio. It was time to prepare for the second night where real challenge awaited. Upon reaching Howard Creek, everyone bundled up for the cold winds. The crew prepared quesadillas, grilled cheese, and chocolate from Linda's daughters. Ultraholic power napped. He got his groove back and set pace. Meanwhile, Coco's heart rate wouldn't slow down. Another break resulted at Nordhoff Ridge. A couple of runners passed and informed 10:00 pm cutoff had just been enforced at Rose Valley. Previous announcements confirmed no cutoffs. Dazed and confused, the Team lost composure. Farther down the road, Happy Meal came over to confirm. The crew argued but to no avail said Happy Meal. BenWah turned off his flashlights and walked like a beaten boxer until Rose Valley.

While awaiting appeal, Red Rock race director, Luis Escobar offered BenWah and Castaway soup and beef tri tips. Verdict arrived. The Team was allowed to continue but warned no aid for the last 23 miles. "You're on your own", said Mauricio. Before leaving, Leap Frog decided to DNF.

Ultraholic DNFd too. Team should have assessed each other's condition before arriving Rose Valley. Five members remained in the hunt for the buckle led by Castaway, Jumpin' J and BenWah. Farther back, Buckle Hoarder stayed with Coco Pimp. Tik, tik, tik, the trio kept checking their watch with no signs of the duo at Chief Peak. When they did, Coco was at her lowest moment.

The four took turns in keeping Coco back to her game. The moon was bright yet nobody paid attention. Jumpin' J saw bonfire from afar meaning there was still life. The four sat down and took nap at lawn chairs. BenWah sat on the ground but was not able to sleep. A sign on the road noted 3.2 miles to trailhead. Topa Topa was just around the corner then. Let's go! About an hour past, not a single sign of a gate appeared. BenWah got impatient and sleep walked to danger. Jumpin' J pulled him away from the edge of fire road. Castaway suggested jogging slowly to break the rhythm. Second sunrise arrived timely as the gate appeared. Topa Topa, here we climb.

Castaway and BenWah motored their way up for another 3.8 miles. Coco Pimp was back to normal and commented the two oldest runners have been leading all the way. BenWah protested against "age" issue. We're only six miles to finish. The race director, Senor Buffoon hasn't left Lion's Canyon Aid Station yet. He was elated to witness for the first time a group of runners intact from the start. Now, go up the final climb to Topa Topa summit with your rocks. Each runner carried a rock to the summit in honor of late ultrarunner, Vikki de Vita who succumbed to cancer two years ago. "I'm so hungry", said BenWah. Let's get our buckle before noon.

Off they traversed single track rolling hills of Lion's Canyon. Castaway and BenWah led and waited on top of a boulder. Two miles to the finish, Leap Frog appeared in sight. He found out that the cutoff time was meant as a joke. 44, 45 hours, it really didn't matter anymore. What about next year?

The Runners:
1) "Coco Pimp" – Carmela Layson
2) "Castaway" – Wilson Liu
3) "Jumpin' J" – Jack Cheng
4) "Buckle Hoarder" – Jakob Herman
5) "Ben Wah Balz" – Ben Gaetos
6) "Leap Frog" – Tin Tse
7) "Ultraholic" – Ted Liao
8) "Happy Meal" – Donn Ozaki

The Crew:
1) Gus Alvarez – Carmela's husband
2) Linda Herman and daughters – Jakob's family

Race Officials:
1) Senor Buffoon – Chris Scott, race director
2) Mauricio Puerto – Aid Station volunteer
3) Luis Escobar – Aid Station volunteer

Ben Gaetos

Chapter 21: Shadow of the Giants 50k

Fish Camp, CA
June 2, 2012

Excitement soared in the air as runners lined up for 23rd staging of Shadow of the Giants 50k Run near Yosemite. Race director, Baz Hawley promised the race to be "magic" with favorable weather. Knowing him, I know he won't disappoint.

Just seconds after the start, the excitement turned into a heart pounding sound of runners gasping for thin air of Sierra National Forest. The course altitude ranged from 5000 ft. – 6300 ft. As course newbie, I opted to remain near the back of the pack. There's plenty of running to do. Be calm and let the body adjust to the altitude. My friend, Drew whom I carpooled gave me brief description of the course mainly on not getting lost.

A short out and back section of the course where 50k / 20k split showed glimpse of the early leaders. A trio of runners led by previous champ, Oswaldo Lopez spearheaded the pack. Women's division was led by newcomer Maria Rivera. After six miles, the course started to gradually descend for 2.5 miles to Big Sandy River crossing. Water was about one foot deep but fun to run through. Thereafter, my senses were awakened to start moving swiftly.

It was always a welcome feeling seeing Baz meet runners wherever possible to give them encouraging words. Course was exceptionally marked with striped ribbons or heavy flour arrow signs. Entering single trail at Mile 13.4 Aid Station, the scenery stepped up its level of interest while going uphill again. Prior, the course was mainly dirt roads bordered by needle pine trees. We would later come back to the same aid station after a big loop of about eleven miles.

The single trail called Nelder Grove directed to a gigantic sequoia tree nicknamed Grand Old Dad. A good downhill section followed albeit technical. Let the shoes do the talking. Voila! I was running on high gear. I wondered where the name of the race originated. My question was quickly answered by the next aid station. The course ran through one mile single trail called Shadow of the Giants Loop. This trail is populated with 3000+ year old giant sequoia trees. At times, I can't hold myself to stop and read quickly about the history of a particular tree. Sightseeing tour done, it was time to figure out what finish time to look for with ten miles left. I was told that it's a little more than five miles of uphill dirt road then off to the finish. I'd be happy with a 6 hrs 15 min finish and much happier to break 6 hours. Let's go get it!

The long ascent was wearisome yet I passed or switched places with a handful of runners. GPS watch was helpful enough to keep me within target pace. Keep moving, keep moving, you'll reel back that runner again, I whispered to myself until I reached the peak. To my surprise, the downhill I longed for was only gradual compared to steep elevation profile. Still, a shot of breaking six hours was reachable. The last aid station volunteers informed me 3.5 miles left to the finish. I still have plenty of gas in my tank. Now, run!

As soon as I saw the direction arrows leading to a single trail, the finish was just a sprint away. Truly, magic was in the air as I crossed the finish line in 5:54:47.

Chapter 22: Long Beach Marathon

City of Long Beach, CA
October 7, 2012

What or who inspired you to run? This question has been asked frequently to every runner. Unlike big city marathons where famed international elite runners headlined the event, Long Beach Marathon top billed the real day to day heroes of the sport.

For headliner, Deo Jaravata ran his 300th marathon. Yes, you read it right, 300 marathons. He ran 52 marathons last year which is equivalent to one every week. By the way, he has full time job as high school teacher at Granada Hills, CA. In an interview, Deo said, "The worst part of a marathon is getting up." Deo wore pink shirt and red tutu skirt. With 300 marathons, he is entitled to wear anything he wanted. Another runner, Marina White also set Guinness Book of World Record for being the youngest female to complete 100 marathons. She's in her 20s.

Deo and Marina were just a couple of runners with amazing stories. Along the way, there were several more individuals who exemplified their toughness and strong will. One wheelchair participant had a sign that read, "Please don't push me."

These are the type of individuals who inspired me to run from single digit distance to the level of 100 mile ultramarathon. My goal for LBM was to finish under 4:30:00. If sub 4 hours was within reach I would go for it. Just make sure

I don't empty my gas tank for upcoming bigger races in my race calendar.

The first eight miles were tightly packed. I weaved myself within tiny gaps along the shore line boardwalk and bike path along the beach. The course was scenic but at times, stop and go traffic from slower runners and walkers. Once the race entered city streets, it was all for the takers. Temperature was warmer than usual. It didn't bother me but some runners were tended by paramedics on roadside.

Residents gave runners big cheers, water, sliced oranges, bananas and hand slaps. California State University Long Beach students welcomed runners with music and cheer leaders as they entered the campus about Mile 17. I passed by another amazing runner, Steve Harvey. He is a legacy runner i.e. he has run all twenty eight Long Beach Marathons. I didn't dare ask his age.

Course was pretty much flat except for a few inclines at bridges and inside CSULB campus. Crowd was lively albeit small compared to Los Angeles Marathon. At ultramarathons, it's an oasis to see even a single spectator along the course. My senses spiked when I caught up with Deo around Mile 22. He was on his way to the Filipino community tent where they served traditional roasted pig. Where else would a fellow Filipino go? After a brief chat with him, I continued my way to the finish. Sub 4 hour finish was already out of reach two miles prior.

As Downtown Long Beach approached, half and full marathon runners merged again. Finish line festivity was just around the corner and would eventually finish in 4:12:20.

Whether you are a veteran, newbie or simply spectator, the excitement can be felt from each individual.

How does it feel? You'll never know until you try.

Ben Gaetos

Chapter 23: Grand Canyon Rim2Rim2Rim Adventure

Grand Canyon, Arizona
October 20, 2012

"Never again", I said to myself as I plodded the trails to the top of South Kaibab Trail of Grand Canyon. I've uttered these words numerous times during races. Was this my final answer?

Grand Canyon is a picturesque place to be. Along with running buddies, Drew and Jay, we drove eight hours from Los Angeles, camped and slept two hours for a midnight start. To complete South Kaibab-North Kaibab-South Kaibab route aka as Rim2Rim2Rim, midnight start or earlier is advisable for daylight finish. Jay ventured last year in 15 hours. Drew and I are neophytes.

A warning sign stated, "Do not attempt to hike from the canyon rim to the river in one day". That distance is only seven miles from top of South Kaibab at Elevation 6800 feet to the river at Elevation 2400 feet. Our plan called 22+ miles one way to North Kaibab then back in 16 hours.

The long quad buster run on uneven erosion control barriers down to Colorado River previewed what challenges we would face at the finish. Bottom neared as the sound level of Colorado River current increased. It was time to refill water at Phantom Ranch.

Darkness still prevailed as we crossed several bridges. We caught up with another runner at Cottonwood Campground.

We saw his flashlights afar. Hikers actually camped to break their journey. Not us, we're going one shot.

Pace was still decent as we ascended North Kaibab with looming sunrise. We bumped into another runner who started from opposite direction. She seemed aware and asked what time we started our R2R2R. A few minutes later, bus loads of runners / hikers descended Colorado River and beyond. Excitement surfaced as the magnificent Grand Canyon landscape became visible.

Time was 7:10am when we reached windy and cold North Kaibab at 8200 feet elevation. Drew and I refilled our hydration pack, added extra layer of clothing and gloves and ran down immediately. Jay wasn't far behind. Drew and I pushed the pace to offset cold. Our eyes were in awe as sedimentary rock formations stood upfront and beyond. North Kaibab's six miles of cliff hanging trail was more runner friendly than South Kaibab.

Another refuel, and off to nine miles of rolling hills along meandering Colorado River followed. Foot traffic was busy as hikers queued their way and stopped for photos. I felt hungry and planned to buy sandwich at Phantom Ranch before the final climb. Energy gels and trail mix weren't enough fuel for this long journey. To my disbelief, I only had $1.50 and can't buy anything. Drew forgot to pack sandwich either. It was almost noon and getting warmer. There were no signs of Jay but we all agreed to wait at the finish.

The long climb began with crossing historic Black Bridge. Drew and I began our snail pace on unending switchbacks and Stairway to Heaven big steps. Dusts whirled occasionally.

Never again, never again, I uttered. Several hikers stopped to admire the view. I just wanted to finish. A few asked where and time I started and received shocking response. When the warning sign re-appeared, I knew the summit neared. Slapping of high fives from finishers erased the tough 46 miles in15 hours, 10 minutes. Doing that made me forget momentarily how tough the course was.

Will I do it again? Let me phone a friend for my final answer.

Chapter 24: Chimera 100 Mile Mountain Race

Cleveland National Forest, Santa Ana Mountains
Lake Elsinore, CA
November 17-18, 2012

The sign read, "Moderation has its place. It ain't here." Chimera is a Greek mythology fire breathing part mountain lion, goat, and serpent. Ultrarunner vs. beast. Fight!

The first twenty miles of Candy Store Loop navigated out and back rocky single trails and root strewn eroded hills of San Juan Trail. A blazing strategy early gives the beast advantage. Wilson, Jack and I have conservative plans. Few followed and kept pace.

Temperature was cool and cloudy with chance of rain late afternoon. This made the climb to Main Divide less strenuous. Are you ready to rock Trabuco Trail downhill? Not yet. One erroneous step in this gnarly graveled narrow trail with thorny bushes can mean free fall hundreds of feet below. Our small group didn't bite at Chimera's trap and preceding miles until Holy Jim Trail at Mile 38.5. The next seven miles of steep uphill tested our climbing prowess. Rain arrived as predicted. We brought poncho and jacket, no problem.

To some, Bear Springs Aid Station was end of their journey. It was dark and about 6 pm. Beaten runners sat and awaited ride to Blue Jay Camp. Our trio was still intact and 3-1/2 hours ahead of cutoff. Downhill preceded. Chance to pad cushion time fell off as low fogs and rain made it difficult to see with eyeglasses. As long as I could hang with the duo, I wouldn't be directionally challenged. The next aid station, Maple Springs at Mile 52.5 housed the only drop bag station. In unpredictable weather, over preparedness may or may not help. I couldn't find things due to tightly packed bag. Heaters at aid stations kept runners warm. I questioned my sanity for running. Aid stations provided hot soup, quesadilla and grilled cheese sandwich at night. Tireless volunteers bundled themselves too.

Downhill rocky jeep road and puddles hit bottom at Silverado Canyon Mile 59.50. Party was over. It was time to ascend unending 14 miles to Upper Holy Jim bypassing Santiago Peak at 5600 feet. There were a couple of aid stations in between to refuel and eat. During the climb, I started dry heaving but my legs were ok. Thus, I was able to cling with Wilson and Jack.

Volunteers at UHJ, asked if I have pacer. I replied that the three of us will stick together. The race director had just altered the course to stay along Main Divide due to mountain lion sighting. Rain was on and off until downpour dropped around 3:30 am. Sleep deprived, I lost track of the duo. They caught up just before Indian Truck Trail. Runners will be at this station at Mile 75.80 and 89.80. I sat down wearily and doubted myself. "Fight, you need this." I kept uttering. I left the aid station first as daylight neared. What comes down must come up. This stretch was mentally defeating. The appearance of double rainbows gave me second life plus news that our friends and pacers will be at the turnaround. After a brief rest, chat and solid foods, we were ready to get our buckle. "Keep going," Jack ordered.

So close yet so far. Chimera kept fighting. The beast kept breathing down our neck with short steep hills in the last ten miles. With three miles left and downhill our pacers, Tin and Jason encouraged us to finish in sub 31 hours and we did.

Chimera has been tamed...only for now.

Chapter 25: Bandit 50k Trail Run

Simi Valley, CA
February 17, 2013

It's a tough course. You'll love it. That was the only description given by a friend who trains at Rocky Peak Mountain, the site of Bandit 50k Trail Run.

Weather forecast called out a high 74F temperature. At the race check in, temperature was chilly. Jacket or no jacket? That was the question. Eventually, the latter prevailed at the last minute. After the first two miles of the race, my body temperature began to rise. The course began climbing a series of steep switchback single trail. I immediately checked my cheat sheet showing elevation profile. The chart indicated about four continuous steep miles to the top. My friend was right. I better run this race smartly.

The highest point, Rocky Peak is popular for hiking and mountain biking. Top elevation is 2715 feet and offers panoramic view of San Fernando Valley and Simi Valley. The name was derived from its large cragged sandstone boulders. The climb itself is a major test of an individual's cardiovascular fitness.

It was music to my ears when I heard cowbells indicating aid station at Mile 5.6. A good single trail downhill section followed. It was time to go fishing i.e. reel back some runners. Mercury was starting to boil. I made sure I was hydrating properly before the next aid station at Mile 9. From here on, it was a roller coaster ride of short hills. Angeles Crest 100

115

champ, Chris Price was on his way back followed by a long train of chasing runners.

By midpoint aid station, runners made their way back. Volunteers who are ultrarunners themselves reminded runners to hydrate and take care of their nutrition needs. The next aid station was another five miles. Better load up. Menu included boiled potatoes, salted pretzels, chocolate cookies, chips, bananas and oranges. Runners exchanged encouraging words or hand slaps at out and back sections.

Approaching Mile 20, big climb loomed on the horizon. Rocky Peak, here we go again. Aid station was well timed for refueling. Aside from foods, they have much needed ice to dip my hat. Thank you. The climb was gradual and runnable initially. Some runners took their chance and went. I didn't and kept my reserved fuel. Happy faces in Hawaiian theme greeted runners at Mile 25 Aid Station. I upped my sugar level with a double dose of soda and chocolate cookie. Pumped up, I'm coming home.

There were still a few climbs but not as strenuous which enabled to pick up weary runners. Running a race is akin to gambling. Take your chance early and hope to have something left at the end or be conservative early and apply reserved energy towards the end. I bet on the latter and began receiving dividends. A quick refill of water at Mile 28 and I was ready for takeoff. But, hold it a second, the final miles to the finish was a downhill free fall. As technical as it could be, Rocky Peak stood by its name, rough, rugged, and jagged. One misstep of eye and foot coordination can mean a bloody fall. Fortunately, I was at my best stride and alerted runners ahead when making a pass.

True to my friend's description of the race, it's a tough course and I loved it. I can't wait for next year.

Chapter 26: Mt. Whitney One Day Hike

Mt. Whitney, CA
September 14, 2013

Killer hike! This was unanimous consensus of everyone who had ventured the famed, Mt. Whitney. The peak at 14,508 feet is the highest summit in the contiguous United States or the lower 48 states. The only mountains higher than Mt. Whitney are in Alaska.

My original plan to hike Mt. Whitney was after completion of Badwater 135 Miles in July. It was traditional to summit the original finish after the race. Ankle injury prevented me from the hike. However, a small group of Los Angeles City employees and I secured a lottery spot for a day hike permit for September. Permits are scarce because of its popularity. The US Forest Service and National Park Service limit the number of hikers on the trail for safety reasons. The most popular route is from Mt. Whitney Portal with a total distance of 22 miles round trip. For the more adventurous, there is also a mountaineer's route and one for the rock climbers.

Our group was composed of Richard and his son David, Henry, Drew and I. Richard and his son have recently hiked Half Dome in Yosemite, CA. David is a top athlete and will compete for a spot in the Olympic swimming team. Henry had hiked Mt. Whitney twice and regularly hikes Mt. Baldy and San Jacinto Mountains in San Bernardino, CA. Drew and I run ultramarathons.

119

We left campground at 2:35 a.m. and drove short minutes to Mt. Whitney Portal trailhead. Due to unknown conditions, we packed heavily with water, foods, jacket, and first aid. It drizzled the night before and weather forecast called for chance of rain showers.

Effect of altitude like headache kicked in immediately at Elevation 8360 feet. Trail was well marked navigating through single trail switchbacks and timber crossings. The ascent time for a day hike is normally 7-8 hours on moderate pace. Knowing the difficulty of the hike, we were in no time pressure at all. If it takes 10 hours, so be it. We took our time and rest whenever needed. Daylight hit us near Trail Camp where most hikers set up tents.

Trail Camp offered scenic panoramic view of Death Valley and High Sierras. It was perfect time to eat breakfast and refill water from Mirror Lake. Drew brought his filtration pump and filled up extra water. Some people suggested water coming out from the rocks on the next 99 switchbacks is good to drink because they have been filtered through sand. What if there is no water? Drew did the right thing by relying on what was available. We can always stash water somewhere along the route.

After a much needed rest, the challenge stepped its ante. Trail ahead was rocky and steep. Henry said he counted 99 switchbacks in his last hike. The summit overlooked us and its spires appeared intimidating. Headache and shortness of breath due to thin air continued. We stopped briefly as needed. Young David at 16 years of age led the assault while the rest of us were a few steps back. I lost count on the number of switchbacks.

Trail Crest at Elevation 13,600 feet was another perfect rest stop for its panoramic view. We're almost there but not really. After a short downhill, a sign read "Mt. Whitney 1.9". This is also a junction for hikers coming or proceeding to the famed John Muir Trail. Some backpackers leave their packs to lighten their load going to the summit. The problem is squirrels or marmots come out in between rocks and feast on hiker's food supply.

That distance marker was misleading as the summit hut appeared still far away. My Garmin GPS indicated a much shorter distance left. The treacherous climb was unending. My hands even hurt from too much pressure on trekking poles. Sign of relief arrived as the hut appeared in clear view. We reached the summit with elapsed time of around 9 hours. Yay, we're on top of the world!

Descending was less pressure. I took off my jacket and switched to running shorts. Return is much faster with fewer stops. Surprisingly, some SoCal ultrarunners were also present during the hike to include Angeles Crest 100 Mile winner, Chris Price and his wife. It was so nice to exchange few words with them. Clouds appeared to darken. The last place you want to be in thunderstorm or lightning is to be exposed in the summit or anywhere in the trails. Thus, we picked up our pace. Rocks could be slippery if it rained. There were already snow spots on the ground and snowflakes in the air. Big group of multi-day hikers were also heading up to Trail Camp.

Finally, we reached Mt. Whitney Portal safely just before 5 pm for an elapsed time of 14 hours. Most importantly, rain poured at the parking area. "Let's get back to our hotel, clean up, eat dinner and have a drink." What else can you ask for?

I Dreamed, I Ran, I Conquered

Chapter 27: Calico 50k Trail Run

Calico Ghost Town, Yermo, CA
January 26, 2014

No excuses! This race was tougher than I thought. Felt like a ghost kicked me in my behind.

Now on its 10th year, I have never considered signing up for this race due to its proximity in schedule with a favorite 50 mile race. In its inception, Calico 50 was scheduled day after Avalon 50 Mile Benefit Run. Schedule has now been moved two weeks apart which attracted more SoCal runners.

Race started and finished at Calico Ghost Town and mining town in the Mojave Desert of San Bernardino County. Calico used to be California's largest silver mining producer. Walter Knott of the famed Knott's Berry Farm purchased the property in the 50s and restored the buildings to its 1880s Western Architecture. Today, the town is flocked by tourists, campers and ATV (All-Terrain Vehicle) enthusiasts.

Weather was favorable in the low to mid 60s. The first two miles were on paved downhill to the lowest point of the race at a shade under 2000 feet elevation. That was easy conversation pace, right? As soon as the course directed to desert sand trail, huffing and puffing sound played to the beat. The tight packed runners spread out quickly as running through deep sand began to take toll. To make it worse, the course was steady uphill battle. One runner asked, how far is the aid station? Nothing was in sight until Mile 6.8.

The next aid station was about 5 miles according to the

125

race volunteer. Footing on the ground was more stable sandy gravel with looming view of hills for the late stages of the race. My pace picked up a little but not for long. I couldn't hold a steady pace. Along mid-way of the race, my split was 3:05:00. It didn't look too good. Major climbs and technical sections still have to be tackled. Passing Aid Station #3 at 17.2 Miles, the highest point of the race at 4000 feet+ elevation was a mile away. That was much welcomed news.

Yes indeed! The descent was very rocky and spiced with steep geometric angle. Runners ahead turned to complete halt wary of their foot landing. I passed without hesitation when clear. As the trail turned between red sandy rock hills, the view of the valley was in superlative degree. A medical aid station was perfectly located to tend bloodied runners. Shotgun bullet shells were also all over the course from target shooting. Bang! Loud thundery sound echoed one after another. My pace was decent but was not gaining much ground to runners up ahead until the aid station at Mile 21.7.

A little bit winded, race volunteer was apologetic to inform that the next 3.1 miles is gradually uphill. My pace was relegated to a walk trying to clear bloating in my stomach. I suspected the soda but no sense complaining. Just deal with it. "You're not thinking DNF right?" A couple of my friends questioned my faltering speed. When the aid station finally was within reach, I went through without stopping. Self-talk got me moving again for the last six miles. The course traversed rolling terrains with remnants of haunted mining caves and sedimentary rocks.

My legs came back for a strong finish in 6:43:11. No

question, this is a great event, even if I was 10 years late.

Chapter 28: The North Face 100k Baguio

Baguio City, Philippines
May 3-4, 2014

The fourth annual TNF100k Baguio billed itself as the Philippines premier ultramarathon. 340 runners from 18 countries converged to The City of Pines. Four consecutive days of rain can possibly result DNF instead of TNF finish.

3am start didn't matter as pumped up early birds arrived. Race started and finished at former US military base, Camp John Hay. Early part of the race awakened runners immediately as they slipped and slid including myself stepping into overgrown tree roots and muds leading to Eco Trail. Unlike boxing, three knockdown rule was waived. Footing settled as runners entered small village where dogs and roosters crow territorial claim. Crossing a short hanging bridge was another wake up call. Race allowed 30 hours cutoff. Thus, I had ample time to regain my stride.

After replenishing with water and boiled yam at Aid Station #2 (AS#2) Km 18.3, the first major ascent began along steep vegetated ridge and pine trees leading to the town of Ampucao. Course was well marked with flags and courteous marshals. The view at this rolling peak at about 1800 meters (6000 ft.) was absolutely magnificent with pastured cows and rock formations. Forewarned about minimal aid station supplies, I made use of my tiny knowledge of local dialect to purchase sports beverage at mini-stores. A runner and I shared half a bowl of the remaining porridge with small portion of chicken and boiled egg. Philex and other gold mining companies used to proliferate here. Villagers also used hoses to tap mountain spring water.

More excitement developed as the race entered rain forest with downed trees and muddy trails. I finally hit my stride descending through this slope. Marshals halted and directed runners to use a rope connecting trails three stories down and another rope to an elevated rocky section leading to another village. This time, descend was on steep concrete causing quad busting and painful jammed toes to the lowest point of the course at 390 meters (1200 ft.) and AS #5 – Km 54.9.

Runners accessed their drop bags at the famed Kennon Road and rested from the steaming temperature. Marshals checked for mandatory night gears. My eyes popped in front of a long span cable supported hanging bridge and gigantic waterfalls. The 20 km (12 mi) 1800 m (5500 ft.) elevation gain Mount Santo Tomas peak at 2260 meters (7415 ft.) guaranteed skyrocket heart rate. Tapped spring water was welcome replenishment in addition to stream crossings. Dark clouds loomed in the horizon.

Indeed a game changer as pouring rain, thunder and lightning made it difficult to navigate with fogged up eyeglasses. I should have opted for the 50k registration. There was no way for me to finish if the rain continued. Midway aid station inspected runners of limatik bites which is akin to leech. With time still way within cutoffs, rain stopped past the summit. Finish time was not an essence. Just be safe. Easy to say but I was holding dear life on steep muddy single trail downhill ravines. A couple of hanging bridge crossings and runners were off for the final 20km (12mi).

Hard earned finish deserved a hard earned medal. At the end of the day, what mattered most was a successful journey. Live another day.

Chapter 29: Fun Runs

"Do you still run 5k/10k Fun Runs? This is too easy for you now." After having run several marathons and ultramarathons, I've often been asked this question. Speedy legs are now history but occasionally I still join these races. Shorter races require more heart pumping action compared to slower pace at ultramarathons for extended period of time.

Race bib numbers served as wall paper in the hallway of our previous house. Every bib has its own story and there are more than 150 short stories behind those bibs. My late friend, Hervey's pet and supply shop may have several citations from the County Health Department for cobwebs in the shop but his back office was grandiose. Each bib and race posters were neatly framed and hung on the wall.

Bib # 854 was my personal best of 42:30 for 10k was set at City of La Canada – Flintridge's Fiesta Days Run on Memorial Day of 1993. This race was loaded with downhill early speeds then rebounded with uphill second half. An ill-advised sub 6 min/mile pace after a mile made me literally crawl the last two miles. The race started and finished inside La Canada's Descanso Gardens.

Los Angeles Chinatown Firecracker Run celebrated Chinese New Year with traditional fireworks and cultural dance. Race traversed into cardiac hilly sections of historic LA Police Academy and Dodger Stadium. Post-race had abundance of food, beer, wine and entertainment. I set my official 5k PR in 1993 with at time of 20:02. For superstitious believers, one year I donned #666.

Half marathons are stepping stone for the big dance i.e. the marathon. It is here where a runner gauges his/her endurance prowess. If only Pheiddipides died running half marathon when he delivered the message about Greek victory over Persia in the Battle of Marathon, running a marathon would be much easier.

Bib #245 marked City of Fontana's Half Marathon which hosted one of the oldest races in the country. Founded in 1955, USA Track and Field recognizes this race as the fastest half marathon in the country. Race starts at Applewhite Campground in Lytle Creek and drops to 2125 feet to finish in front of the City Hall. First half is winding road and the second half is almost a straight slightly downhill along Sierra Road. You can see the finish line from afar but it never gets any closer. I set a half marathon PR of 1:38:00 on this course in 2003.

Buffalo Half Marathon was as scenic as it can be. Catalina Island is in one of my favorite place to run. First half of the hilly race was mostly paved road with incredible views of the island. When I ran the race in 2002, I carried a copy of the course profile. Diagram indicated downhill for the last 5-6 miles. I was ecstatic on what I thought was the summit only to deflate my emotion seeing ant sized runners climbing a distant hill. I grinded every step then regained speed at the turnaround. Next day, I immediately notified the race that their race profile was not correct. Correction was made the following year.

Classic memories remain looking at my bib for Mt. Baldy Run 2 the Top. Most people travel on Labor Day weekend. A few form a beeline towards San Bernardino Mountains for some challenge. Just less than eight miles in total distance from start to finish, runners seek the experience of running at high altitude and thin air on mountain ledge and ridge aptly called Devil's Backbone. Race starts at Elevation 6000 feet and ends at the summit with Elevation 10,064 feet. How do runners get back to their parking? A newbie asked. Runners walk down about 3.5 miles to ride a ski lift or run back to the parking lot. Since it is Labor Day, there is still some time to barbeque at home.

Lastly, Run2 the Top bib has its counterpart named Stair Climb to the Top. Race poster noted "Elevators are for Wimps". Formerly known as Library Tower and First Interstate Building, the 73 story office building is now called U.S. Bank Tower. It is the tallest building in California and tenth tallest in the United States. Participants race up the 1500 steps from ground floor to the roof top. Unlike New York's Empire State Building Stair Climb mass start, Run2 the Top has 2 runners take off every 10 seconds. I participated three times finishing all in under or over 15 minutes. At one time, the event coincided with my daughter's birthday party. After helping out prepare food ingredients, I still had time to participate in the stair climb and be back to the house.

For now, those running bibs are packed in a binder. One bib, one story, their memories remain.

Ben Gaetos

Chapter 30: For the Record

These days, the list of races continues to grow. Beginners and veteran runners have variety of choices from a short 5k fun run to a classic 100 mile ultramarathon. Choosing a race is like comparing apples and oranges. The good ones sell out faster than a blink of an eye the moment registration opens up. The popularity of ultramarathon has increased that it has now become the new 26.2.

In my first eight years of running, I concentrated on shorter distances and 1-2 marathons a year. Speed was the name of the game. After retiring my running shoes briefly, I came back with new lease in life. As of this writing, below are official list of 61 ultramarathons and 58 marathons I have completed.

1) Los Angeles Marathon – March 1, 1992
2) Los Angeles Marathon – March 7, 1993
3) Los Angeles Marathon – March 6, 1994
4) Los Angeles Marathon – March 5, 1995
5) Los Angeles Marathon – March 3, 1996
6) Santa Clarita Marathon - Nov. 9, 1996
7) Los Angeles Marathon - March 2, 1997
8) Los Angeles Marathon – March 29, 1998
9) Los Angeles Marathon – March 14, 1999
10)   Los Angeles Marathon – March 5, 2000
11)   Long Beach Marathon – Nov. 12, 2000
12)   Western Hemisphere Marathon, Culver City – Dec. 13, 2000

13) Los Angeles Marathon – March 4, 2001
14) Catalina Marathon – March 17, 2001
15) Portland Marathon – Oct. 7, 2001
16) Santa Clarita Marathon – Nov. 4, 2001
17) Los Angeles Marathon – March 3, 2002
18) Catalina Marathon – March 16, 2002
19) Bulldog 50k Trail Run, Malibu, CA – Sept. 7, 2002
20) Long Beach Marathon – Oct. 13, 2002
21) Los Angeles Marathon – March 2, 2003
22) Catalina Marathon – March 15, 2003
23) Bulldog 50k Trail Run, Malibu, CA - Sept. 6, 2003
24) Avalon 50 Mile Benefit Run, Catalina Island – Jan. 20, 2004
25) Pacific Shoreline Marathon, Huntington Beach, CA – Feb. 1, 2004
26) Los Angeles Marathon – March 7, 2004
27) Catalina Marathon – March 13, 2004
28) Bulldog 50k Trail Run, Malibu, CA – Aug. 24, 2004
29) Santa Clarita Marathon – Nov. 7, 2004
30) California International Marathon, Sacramento, CA – Dec. 5, 2004
31) Pacific Shoreline Marathon, Huntington Beach, CA – Feb. 5, 2005
32) Los Angeles Marathon – March 6, 2005
33) Catalina Marathon – March 19, 2005
34) Volcano Wilderness Marathon, Volcano, HI – July 30, 2005
35) Mt. Disappointment 50k Endurance Run, Mt. Wilson, CA – Aug. 13, 2005

36) Bulldog 50k Trail Run, Malibu, CA – Aug. 27, 2005

37) Santa Clarita Marathon – Nov. 6, 2005

38) OTHTC 50k Ultramarathon, Ridgecrest, CA – Dec. 4, 2005

39) Orange Curtain 50k Run , Cerritos, CA – Feb. 18, 2006

40) Catalina Marathon – March 18, 2006

41) Los Angeles Marathon – March 19, 2006

42) Leona Divide 50 Mile Trail Run, Lake Hughes, CA – April 22, 2006

43) Palos Verdes Marathon – May 20, 2006

44) Mt. Disappointment 50k Endurance Run, Mt. Wilson, CA – Aug. 12, 2006

45) Bulldog 50k trail Run, Malibu, CA – Aug. 26, 2006

46) San Diego 100 Mile Endurance Run – Oct. 21-22, 2006

47) Pacific Coast Trail Run, Pt. Mugu, CA – Nov. 19, 2006

48) Avalon 50 Mile Benefit Run, Catalina Island – Jan. 13, 2007

49) Orange Curtain 50k Run, Cerritos, CA – Feb. 17, 2007

50) Los Angeles Marathon – March 4, 2007

51) Catalina Marathon – March 17, 2007

52) Leona Divide 50 Mile Trail Run, Lake Hughes, CA – April 21, 2007

53) Wild, Wild West 50k Trail Run, Lone Pine, CA – May 2007

54) Holcomb Valley 33 Mile Trail Run, Big Bear Lake,

CA – June 10, 2007

55) Mt. Disappointment 50k Endurance Run, Mt. Wilson, CA – Aug. 11, 2007

56) Bulldog 50k Trail Run, Malibu, CA– Aug. 25, 2007

57) Angeles Crest 100 Mile Endurance Run – Sept. 16-17, 2007

58) Santa Clarita Marathon – Nov. 4, 2007

59) Avalon 50 Mile Benefit Run, Catalina Island – Jan. 12, 2008

60) Death Valley Trail Marathon, Death Valley, CA – Feb. 3, 2008

61) Orange Curtain 50k Run, Cerritos, CA – Feb. 16, 2008

62) Catalina Marathon – March 15, 2008

63) Leona Divide 50 Mile Trail Run, Lake Hughes, CA – April 19, 2008

64) Palos Verdes Marathon – May 17, 2008

65) Holcomb Valley 33 Mile Trail Run, Big Bear Lake, CA – June 8, 2008

66) Mt. Disappointment 50 Mile Endurance Run, Mt. Wilson, CA – Aug. 8, 2008

67) Angeles Crest 100 Mile Endurance Run – Sept. 23-24, 2008

68) Santa Clarita Marathon – Nov. 2, 2008

69) Catalina Eco-Marathon, Catalina Island – Nov. 15, 2008

70) Rose Valley 33 Mile Endurance Run, Ojai, CA – Nov. 29, 2008

71) Diamond Valley Lake Marathon, Hemet, CA – Jan.

24, 2009

72) Bataan Death March 52k Test Run, Philippines – Feb. 22, 2009

73) Catalina Marathon – March 14, 2009

74) Pasadena Marathon – March 21, 2009

75) Old Goats 50 Mile Trail Run, Lake Elsinore, CA – March 28, 2009

76) Leona Divide 50 Mile Trail Run, Lake Hughes, CA – April 18, 2009

77) Palos Verdes Marathon – May 2, 2009

78) San Diego 100 Mile Endurance Run – June 6-7, 2009

79) Long Beach Marathon – Oct. 11, 2009

80) Saddleback Trail Marathon – Nov. 7, 2009

81) Santa Clarita Marathon – Nov. 8, 2009

82) Chimera 100k Trail Run, Lake Elsinore, CA – Dec. 12, 2009

83) Avalon 50 Mile Benefit Run, Catalina Island – Jan. 24, 2010

84) Bataan Death March 102k, Philippines – March 7, 2010

85) Los Angeles Marathon – March 21, 2010

86) Old Goats 50 Mile Trail Run, Lake Elsinore, CA – March 27, 2010

87) Palos Verdes Marathon – May 15, 2010

88) San Diego 100 Mile Endurance Run – June 12-13, 2010

89) Angeles Crest 100 Mile Endurance Run – Aug. 28-29, 2010

90) Spooner's Cove 50k Trail Run, Montana de Oro,

CA– Nov. 20, 2010

91) Avalon 50 Mile Benefit Run, Catalina Island, CA – Jan. 15, 2011

92) Catalina Marathon – March 12, 2011

93) Los Angeles Marathon – March 20, 2011

94) Old Goats 50 Mile Trail Run, Lake Elsinore, CA – March 26, 2011

95) Leona Divide 50 Mile Run, Lake Hughes, CA – April 30, 2011

96) Bishop High Sierra 50 Miles, Bishop, CA – May 21, 2011

97) Angeles Crest 100 Mile Endurance Run – July 23-24, 2011

98) Bulldog 50k Trail Run, Malibu, CA – Aug. 27, 2011

99) Chino Hills 50k, Chino Hills, CA – Oct. 1, 2011

100) Saddleback Trail Marathon, Lake Elsinore, CA - Nov. 5, 2011

101) Chimera 100k Trail Run, Lake Elsinore, CA– Nov. 19, 2011

102) Avalon 50 Mile Benefit Run, Catalina Island, CA – Jan 14, 2012

103) Bataan Death March 160k Ultramarathon – Philippines – Jan. 28-29, 2012

104) Coyote 2 Moon 100 Miles, Ojai, CA – Mar. 9-11, 2012

105) Orange County Marathon, Newport Beach, CA – May 5, 2012

106) Shadow of the Giants 50k Trail Run, Fish Camp, CA – June 2, 2012

107) Mt. Disappointment 33 Mile Endurance Run, Mt Wilson, CA – Aug. 11, 2012

108) Bulldog 50k Trail Run, Malibu, CA – Aug. 25, 2012

109) Long Beach Marathon, Long Beach, CA – October 7, 2012

110) Saddleback Trail Marathon, Lake Elsinore, CA - Nov.3, 2012

111) Chimera 100 Mile Mountain Race, Lake Elsinore, CA – Nov. 17-18, 2012

112) Winter 7 Series Marathon (Day 7) – Long Beach, CA – December 20, 2012

113) Avalon 50 Mile Benefit Run – Catalina Island, CA – Jan. 12, 2013

114) Surf City Marathon – Huntington Beach, CA – Feb. 3, 2013

115) Bandit 50k Trail Run – Simi Valley, CA – Feb. 17, 2013

116) Old Goats 50 Miles – Lake Elsinore, CA – March 23, 2013

117) Badwater 135 Mile Ultramarathon – Death Valley, CA – July 15-17, 2013

118) Avalon Benefit 50 Mile Run – Catalina Island – Jan. 11, 2014

119) Calico 50k Trail Run – Calico Ghost Town, Yermo, CA – Jan. 26, 2014

120) The North Face 100k Baguio – Baguio City, Philippines – May 3-4, 2014

Ben Gaetos

Chapter 31: The Road to Badwater

I heard it through the grapevine.

The first time I heard about Badwater Ultramarathon was when Steve Matsuda from Ultraladies and Men Running Club ran in 2002. 50k (31 miles) ultramarathon was all new to me. To fathom 135 miles was out of this world.

The following year, Pam Reed of Arizona and Dean Karnazes of California relived the Battle of the Sexes. Pam Reed prevailed. Thereafter, I followed the race religiously. In 2006, seven times Western States 100 Mile Endurance Run winner, Scott Jurek defended his Badwater 135 title. A year before, Jurek set a course record 24:36:08. A sub-24 hour finish was knocking on the door. However, Jurek was not the headliner of the race. Unheralded rookies, Akos Konya from Hungary and U.S. Navy Seal, David Goggins spiced up the race. Both Konya and Goggins started in the 6:00 am wave while Jurek joined the elite runners in the 10:00 am wave. Konya crossed the finish line first. Jurek who started four hours behind Konya had the least aggregate time by 17 minutes and proclaimed winner. Goggins finished fifth overall.

Badwater became more interesting when LA's top ultrarunner, Jorge Pacheco entered the race in 2007. I followed the race updates all night. Brazil's Vladimir Nunez won and set the current course record of 22:51:29. Jorge rebounded with a win in 2008 and captured Ultrarunning Magazine's Ultrarunner of the Year Award.

I've seen the DVD, Running on the Sun which is a

documentary about Badwater 135. The movie wasn't enough. I wanted to see the action live. The late, Hervey Chapman joined me in 2009 to watch the race. That was an electrifying experience. On our way home, Hervey observed my keen interest in the race. He offered to sponsor majority of my expense in case I decide to run Badwater. Nancy Shura-Dervin had been pitching the race to me too. I was scared and not ready yet.

In March 2010, I visited the Philippines and ran Bataan Death March 102K in extreme heat, humidity and dusts on paved road. Sixty three miles of pavement running was a stepping stone to the main goal. An invitation by my friend, Adalberto "Flaco" Mendoza to crew for him at Badwater 135 was welcome opportunity. This gave me real picture of the race. Flaco had previously finished Badwater 135 in 37 hours. Unfortunately, Flaco Did Not Finish (DNF) at Mile 90. My dream also diminished as my main sponsor, Hervey lost his battle with leukemia in 2011. He kept his illness to himself even as it was obvious he was losing a lot of weight. During my wife and I's visit at the hospital, Hervey uttered, "Ben, I still owe you money for LA Marathon and Badwater." "Don't worry about it. Just get well", I replied.

Badwater 135 dream faded thereafter. Meanwhile, Los Angeles based running store, A Runner's Circle offered to support any Filipino runner to receive invitation to this race. No Filipino has ever run Badwater 135. ARC is owned by Filipino entrepreneurs, Joe Matias and Derek Biesheuvel. There are a handful of Filipino ultrarunners in Northern California. My name came up in conversations. With the time limit reduced from 60 hours to 48 hours in 2011, no one took the bait.

My race times continued to improve noticeably. Whatever I was doing must be working well resulting to personal best at Angeles Crest 100 Mile Endurance Run at 31:41:12 in 2011. Nancy convinced me again to apply for Badwater and was unsuccessful.

Year 2012 arrived and improvements continued. Was it the added cross training at the gym or mountain biking? 10:10:25 at Avalon 50 Mile race at Catalina Island was impressive. Two weeks later, my race at Bataan Death March in the Philippines was unbelievable. Longtime dream of sub-24 hour finish in a 100 miler came to fruition at BDM. Another 100 miler in March, Coyote 2 Moon in Ojai, CA plus a sub 4 hour finish at Orange County Marathon in May turned my time clock seven years back. On the night prior to 2012 AC100, Nancy again gave a lengthy talk about Badwater in the presence of my buddy, Drew. Drew was amazed on Nancy's tool box full of blister kit. I DNFd at AC100 but rebounded immediately for my third buckle in a year at Chimera 100 Miles.

In January of 2013, I ran 9:56:25 at Avalon 50 Miler. The result solidified confidence to have a solid shot at Badwater 135. Main concern was raising enough monetary support for Badwater. Mssrs. Jorge Pacheco and John Radich who are both Badwater veterans addressed several of my concerns.

I always thought Badwater 135 was for elites only. Their words and wisdom served inspiration to push my limits.

Ben Gaetos

Chapter 32: Planning 101

"Rome wasn't built in a day." As humongous as it can be, preparation for Badwater required great deal in planning. It needed more than just hope and pray. Key factors in my planning were: 1) Sponsors, 2) Training and preparation, 3) Crew members, and 4) Family support.

Badwater 135 participation wouldn't be possible without assistance from generous sponsors. Badwater veterans gave me ballpark figure of expenditures. My savings wasn't enough to cover the cost. ARC co-owner, Joe Matias was very supportive from the get go. He garnered additional gear product sponsors such as shoes, hydration drinks, flashlights, reflective vests, sunglasses, etc. not only for me but a few things for crew members too. Co-workers, family, relatives, and close friends also pitched in generously. Chief crew, Nancy provided list of emergency and non-emergency supplies. She had been there a few times as runner, medical staff and chief crew. There were no stones unturned in her list including a hammer. Yes, hammer was used to crush ice. Mother knows best. On race day, we were ready for war.

Gluten of punishment was the consensus. Just like school, runner has to do one's homework diligently without shortcuts. Training plans was laid out to simulate race conditions. It was back to the roads again. The long stretch from my house in Eagle Rock, Los Angeles to Mount Lee aka Hollywood Sign was perfect for weekend long runs. There are several convenience stores and water fountains along the way to Griffith Park. The route established my 30 mile long run on

Saturdays. In addition, taking Fridays off from work enabled back to back training days. Mt. Baldy served as altitude training at Elevation 10,064 feet. Many participants attended Death Valley training camp. I devised my own. Key workout was Memorial Day week. I logged 3- 30 milers including trip to Red Rock Canyon, NV. My friends, Dave and June invited me and my friend, Drew to their home in Summerlin, NV. Call it a boot camp. As soon as we arrived, off we went for a run in the desert. Next day, we were off for a morning and afternoon training runs. The roads replicated Mile 0-17 (Badwater to Furnace Creek).

When many Angelenos complained of heat wave in June, I sneaked a run at Cabazon Outlet Stores near Palm Springs. Unfamiliar to the area, I mistakenly entered restricted Indian reservation ground. Security hollered to leave the ground even if there were no structures around. I was only armed with water and electrolyte drink. So as not to waste driving time, I looked for another route near the area. At mid-day and triple digit temperature, motorists including cops gave me strange looks and inquiries such as, "Do you know where you're going? Do you need help? Are you ok?"

Drew was also training for a hot weather race, Angeles Crest 100 Miles. The four mile stretch of Palm Springs Tram Road suited race conditions well. We stashed water midway and at the top. A security officer became wary of our acts. I told security that we were both training for the heat and have stashed water and electrolyte drinks behind bushes. The high 117F temperature delivered clear understanding and adjustments needed.

Other key training factors were daily dry sauna sessions from 20-60 minutes, weight training, stationary bike and treadmill with portable heaters and multiple lights around, and turning car heater even during summer. Gym membership at nearby World Gym in Glendale was inexpensive. Drew followed suit in gym membership.

Crew plays very essential role in any race particularly at Badwater. The runner puts his / her life in their hands. Thus, selection of crew members must be carefully studied. Several runners including one from State of Maryland offered his services. With Nancy as chief crew, I needed perfect chemistry to blend with the group. Tensions among crew members occur in this kind of event. A couple of runners offered to crew for one day only. What if they don't show up? This required proper coordination as phone signal is very limited or none at all at Death Valley. Eventually, final selection was formed. The Team held meetings and communicated via emails or phone calls to follow up on important matters. Nancy had me list down nutrition values of my food intakes. She also gave the crew a lecture on proper hydration and heat raining. We were all students. On race day, we were ready to rock n roll. A sense of unity was felt when we held each other's hands prior to the start of the race to pray for a successful mission.

Finally, participation to Badwater 135 required blessing from my family. My wife, Josie was nervous. Who wouldn't? This race is a matter of life and death against the elements of nature. My daughter, Paula was excited but wary of the dangers. It's difficult but not impossible. My mom was also excited but at the same time nervous. Training required being away long hours. In spite of this, I tried my best to fulfill household obligations I normally do. I only wished I could clone myself.

Ben Gaetos

Chapter 33: Team Ocho

The Dream Team took a lot of decision making to form. Two of my picks couldn't make it due to schedule conflicts. The name, Team Ocho as in Figure 8 came from Rafa for its infinite strength. Rafa, Drew and Jay know each other from races. Sundar and Balmore are new bloods. You can't always get what you want. Still, Team Ocho delivered to the fullest. The following are the members resume.

Nancy Shura-Dervin:
Chief Crew, aka Ultra Mom
Never ran a step before age 40
Marathon finishes: +/- 40 including 4 Boston Marathon finishes
Ultra Marathon finishes: +/- 50 including 2001 Angeles Crest 100 Miles
2003 Badwater Ultra Marathon finisher: 52:35:--
Badwater Crew Chief - 4 times
Badwater Medical Crew – 1 time
Crewed Badwater Double (135 miles x 2 = 270 miles)
Running Coach: Road Runners Club of America
Founder/Coach: UltraLadies Running Club
Race Director: Bulldog 50K Ultra Run, Valley Crest Half Marathon
Business Owner: Trail Run Events, LLC
CA Licensed Nurse
Association: Nancy coached me for my first ultramarathon, Bulldog 50k in 2002. For Badwater 135, there

was no one else I would pick to lead the team. Her husband, Larry and I have worked on construction project for the City of Los Angeles. I was the architect. Larry was the construction superintendent.

Badwater Highlight(s): 1) Yelling at me and my pacer, Jay to slow down. I jumped to a 7:00 min/mile pace at Mile 59 after taking a nap and drinking Coke. 2) After having my feet taped, she told me it was bad luck to take a shower the night before the race. I always take shower before going to bed.

Rafael Covarrubias:

Past races completed: multiple Angeles Crest 100 Miles, 2013 Western States 100 Miles, San Diego 100 Miles, Coyote 2 Moon 100 Miles, Rocky Road 100 Miles, Champion Mileage and Points at SoCal Ultramarathon Grand Prix Series, Avalon 50M, Bishop 100K, Leona Divide 50M, Mt Disappointment 50M, LA Marathon, Long Beach Marathon, etc.

Profession: School teacher

Association: Rafa and I have been on several races together. "Mr. Cool" knows when to make his move at every race.

Badwater Highlight(s): Rafa was always calm as ever even at the time I was hurting badly. I'd be glad to be on his Badwater Team anytime.

Drew Foote:

He is the karate expert, Zen master, adventurer and rock climber among other things.

Past races completed: 3 time finisher Angeles Crest 100

Mile, Coyote 2 Moon 100 Mile, Bishop High Sierra 100k, Mt. Disappointment 50M, Avalon 50M, Long Beach Marathon, Grand Canyon Rim2Rim2Rim Adventure.

Profession: Past work includes digital movie scanner for Sony Pictures, house painter, handyman, and more.

Association: I have known Drew since 2008 while training for Mt. Disappointment and AC100. We have logged so many miles and adventures on the trails together.

Badwater Highlight(s): 1) Two miles into the final 13 mile climb of the race; Drew suggested pulling me off the road to stretch my legs and massage my lower back. I was hurting badly. After that, he asked the team to gather around, hold our hands and generate some energy.

Jay Torres:

Past races completed: Officially 20 Marathons. Unofficially, every weekend training run,

Ultras include Ridgecrest 50k, 2- Old Goats 50M, Grand Canyon Rim2Rim2Rim twice.

Triathlons completed: Two California IronMan70.3, Wildflower 70.3, Magic Mountain Man 70.3.

Profession: "Spaceship Tripper" at JPL-NASA. He is one of NASA's space programmers for the Rover's mission to Mars.

Association: Bumped into Jay with two of my running buddies at Verdugo Mountain in Glendale. He was running solo. Immediately after the run, he emailed to inquire about our next training run.

Badwater Highlight(s): Jay created a link for my

supporters to track me down. The site generated about 4000 followers during the race. He called my family to update my status.

Sundar Vembu:

Past races completed: about 30 half marathons and a couple of marathons, 4- 50Ks, Rock n River 50 Miles and Born to Run 100K. First ultramarathon – Bulldog 50k in 2011

Profession: Software architect for the Southern California Gas Company. He is also an excellent photographer.

Association: When one of crew members remained non-committal, Nancy suggested Sundar to be on the team. Sundar trains with the Ultraladies Club.

Badwater Highlight(s): Sundar was very reserved but knew every trail around the Sierras. He had hiked them all.

Balmore Flores:

Past races completed: ran track and cross country for Hamilton High School, finished 13 marathons including several Los Angeles Marathons, San Diego Rock & Roll Marathons, and Mountain to the Sea Marathon in Ojai, CA.

Trail races completed: Valley Crest Half Marathon - two times, Bulldog 50K, Holcomb Valley 33 miler, Leona Divide 50, Avalon 50, Chimera 100 and Born to Run 100. Dream Race: Hard Rock 100.

Profession: Former Military (US Navy), Graduated from Cal State University in Northridge, CA, works as underwriter for banks and brokers.

Association: Balmore and I met at Chimera 100 Miles in

2012. He is new to ultras but runs like a veteran and deer like speed. Balmore replaced Jay due to last minute work schedule conflict. When Jay notified he was free again, I asked Jay to rejoin the team and still kept Balmore.

Badwater Highlight(s): Balmore kept me going all the time. I did most of my faster splits with him.

Selection of the team members was not based on speed and experience alone. The willingness to work together as a team was key factor. Team Ocho blended well and set aside personality issues that could have risen. On race day, everyone came prepared. I couldn't ask for anything more.

Chapter 34: Badwater 135 Mile Ultramarathon

Death Valley, CA
July 15-17, 2013

"Are you ready? Can you run the whole race? Don't kill yourself; I want to see you back, ok? After responding to these questions the past few weeks, the day has come to find the answer. Runners get set, go!

Overcast clouds deceived several runners to faster than normal pace including me. Front runners were going suicidal 7 minute/mile pace. My six member crew hollered to slow down. Mile 17 checkpoint at Furnace Creek was still far away. I tried to spot locations of Badwater veterans. JR Radich and Marshall Ulrich were behind. Just follow their strategy. Slowly, I began to look around the scenery below sea level such as the colorful rocky mountain Artist's Drive, salt beds and a sign, Devil's Golf Course.

In due time, the heat struck its fury. My crew kept my body cool by repeatedly spraying cold water, iced bandana and cold towel over my cap every mile. In addition, hydration bottles were always ice cold. Palm Springs and sauna training was paying off but dealt with nose bleeding and tooth ache until Mile 41 – Stovepipe Wells.

The main battle occurred at Stovepipe Wells to Townes Pass. I left SPW with new shoes and clothes about 5 pm. Middle part of the shoes melted. I also had naan bread, hummus and Coke. That was a huge mistake. My stomach crumbled processing huge amount of food a few miles into the climb. Flame thrower like headwind forced runners to exert more energy at this 18- mile ascent. Ambient temperature was reported to be 121F while ground temperature reached 180F. Badwater veterans advised just survive first day to have a shot of finishing. My pacer, Balmore reminded me to take my time to get to Townes Pass at Elevation 4956 feet. A reward of downhill waits. Right on, I arrived 15 minutes before midnight. The pre-planned 20 minute nap was very timely. The crew constantly monitored my calorie, sodium, and weight including urine color. I was in very good hands.

Eleven miles of steep downhill separated Mile 72 checkpoint, Panamint Springs. My pacer, Jay ran with me for this much awaited section. After two miles, Jay was summoned by chief crew, Nancy. "Slow down, you guys are running 7 minute/mile." Jay replied, "How can I contain a tiger?" At 3:59am, I checked in at Panamint Springs. Party was over. No more light flashing vehicles to pass. It was time to climb again. The road was not as steep but covered 18 miles of switchbacks. I successfully made it to the top of scenic Darwin Turnoff and most of all out of Death Valley Basin about 10:30am.

Left ankle began to swell at Mile 90. Nancy applied tape immediately. A third pair of shoes one size up was necessary and a fourth came after just a few steps. Left foot was so swollen. Rafa took over pacing duties and had me run one minute and walk one minute. Balmore did the same and set 100 mile as milestone. We did, but pain worsened including lower back. I leaned left like Tower of Pisa.

My pacers alternately suggested ways of correcting my posture. We stopped and stretched, hold water bottle on the right, relaxed my right shoulder, etc. I would be walking straight but not long. Nancy would yell on the van whenever I leaned. The comments began stressing me. I tried my best but it was just too painful. Sundar was calmest of all. He rarely talked but gave excellent power walking tip. Sandstorm blew at full speed. All I can see was a long stretch of road. I was so tired and sleepy as sundown loomed. Where the hell is Lone Pine?

Lone Pine at Mile 122 was second to the last checkpoint. Tourists cheered arrival of runners. I wished it was finish line but biggest challenge threatened i.e. 4600 ft. climb in 13 miles. While eating half a sandwich, I assessed my condition. There were no blisters, leg cramps or stomach issues and still moving in spite of pain. No one can stop me now, let's go.

Jay led the pacing one mile at a time. That was perfect set up as it allowed me to thank each one for this historic moment. Meanwhile, my body was falling apart. My pacers nudged or guided me to keep myself in forward direction. A short break necessitated stretching my back and legs on the ground. Stars were in galactic formation. I asked Drew what were those up above in angled position. He replied, stars. "How come they're moving", I asked. "You mean we're going up there?"

After the last checkpoint, Mile 131 I told my pacer let our friends wait longer. Let me enjoy my victory lap. I quietly prayed and thanked the people who inspired and supported me, people who believed in me led by my chief crew and ultramom Nancy, ARC family, running and non – running friends, co-workers and most of all Filipinos. It was an honor to be first Filipino finisher at Badwater. A historic moment created in 44 hours, 8 minutes and 7 seconds. Thank you to my wife, daughter and family for bearing with me. We did it!

Chapter 35: Why do I run?

When asked, why do I run? It is safe to say for health reasons and relieving stress. It is true, no question about it. Beneath those footprints, ADVENTURE marks every step of the way. Let me show the way.

Automobile is akin to human body. It is the center piece in running. Automobiles require maintenance service every 30,000, 40,000, 50,000 miles, etc. to keep them in good condition for our daily commute and travels. Our body requires the same maintenance as we age. Both can live long and healthy if it is well taken cared. Time and time again. I would learn about someone in serious health condition. In most cases, it was due to abuse of the body from alcohol and eating unhealthy foods. Only at this time will the individual start living healthy i.e. if it is not too late. Coming from a family with chronic history of heart disease in my father side, I made some changes in my lifestyle and started living a healthier life.

Discovering new heights make running more interesting. Finishing a marathon is a daunting accomplishment in itself. But then again, I stepped up to another level. A friend of mine commented, "Ben and I ran 5k together, then a 10k, half marathon and weathered a storm at Catalina Marathon. He got crazy and started to run ultramarathons. No way, I'm following him." Yes, indeed. Once I entered the dark side of ultramarathon, I discovered an entire new world of running. There is no turning back.

Voyage takes on distant places. One of my favorite

television show as a kid was the science fiction, Voyage to the Bottom of the Sea. The nuclear submarine, Seaview ran across several obstacles and battles to reach their destination. Running had its own classic battles too such as terrain, altitude, weather, distance, wildlife, etc. My feet are my mode of transportation to places such Mt. Whitney, Mt. Baldy, and Grand Canyon National Park and to the lowest point in the United States, Badwater in Death Valley and many more. Adventure never ends.

Excellence is what everyone pursues in life. Be the best of what we want to be. Adventure and goals do not stop until the fat lady sings. Being an overachiever is always a positive approach. If running a marathon is easy then everyone would be running. When the runner hits the wall, does the runner continue or stop? This is where the pursuit of excellence surfaces. We bring our best when the chips are down. Running has helped me overcome the "walls" in life.

Nature and its wonders are main ingredients for any adventure. From the mountains to the sea and into the desert, running is never dull whether it is winter, spring, summer or fall. We learn to adapt to changes and use this experience in battles we encounter in our daily life.

Togetherness and camaraderie develop in each adventure. After completing a 100 miler, a runner/friend once quoted, "Where were these folks all my life?" We talked about life, goals, dreams, etc. and encouraged each other at races. The perception that running is an individual sport contradicts the fact that running is actually a team sport. The ultrarunning community is a tight knit group of individuals sharing a common goal.

Ultimate means the farthest point in a journey. As T.S. Elliott quoted, "Only those who risk going too far can possibly find out how far one can go." Some people are contented with what they have and level they are in. They're too afraid of a risk. Others step up to see what they are made of. They are willing to fight the difficult battle. They give up the comfort and go through pain in order to succeed.

Recollection of fun things and war stories after races or adventures are worth sharing. Sharing experiences such as race reports and photos inspire others. This is one way of giving back something to the running community. Where else can you find a group of runners singing birthday song in the middle of a 100 mile race under a full moon?

Ecstasy is the state of overmastering feeling. Some people enjoy movies, shop, drink alcohol, eat out, etc. Mine is the joy in running. It is my solitude away from big city life with no phone calls, traffic and other distractions. Birds, squirrels, river flow, and blowing wind are music to my ears.

When asked the same question again, the answer will almost always be the same. Only the adventure will be different.

Chapter 36: One Shot Dream

"Look, if you had one shot, one opportunity to seize everything you ever wanted one moment, would you capture it or just let it slip?" Eminem's song lyrics perfectly exemplified my quest of Badwater 135.

Post Badwater 135 started with responding to congratulatory calls at 4 am, two hours after crossing the finish line. My wife was happy that I made it to the finish. Drew and I canceled our hike to Mt. Whitney summit due to my injury. We headed home a day early. Interview from The Filipino Channel (TFC) cable television at ARC's Thursday Fun Run followed. Emails and messages from all over kept coming some of whom I don't even know. My success opened the door to many runners. Everyone was scared of the beast. With this advent, several runners expressed interest in participating and requested assistance in their application for the following year. Badwater 135 was widely followed worldwide as 25 countries were represented at the race. Even non-runners religiously followed the webcast.

Many believed Badwater was for elites only when finish cutoff time was reduced to 48 hours in 2011. Battle tested Filipino heritage came into play to overcome the odds. My heart and soul was ready to battle the devil. Prior to my application, I asked several Badwater 135 veterans about strategy, training and logistics. Due to health conditions, Gary Hilliard responded with one word advice; be patient.

It was a great honor to be distinguished as the first Filipino to be invited and complete Badwater 135. The distinction spread out like fire but created little distraction during training. With the advent of the Philippines' running boom, running interest stepped to another notch. There are a number of excellent runners who need international exposure. May they follow the road to Badwater.

More interview requests from Philippine media followed. News spread out through Eagle Rock Community Patch, Asian Journal newspaper, Manila tabloid- Bulgar, sports tv, internet blogs, on-line magazines, Runner's World – Philippines, Frontrunner Magazine, Managing Wealth magazine, Philippine Air Lines' Mabuhay Magazine and live interview via Skype for Sun-Star newspaper. My food likes and dislikes were posted at 100 Miles Café near Manila. To my wife's surprise, my presence was acknowledged by the featured band at the Watermelon Festival held at the Rose Bowl in Pasadena.

I was glad to complete Badwater 135 in 2013. Outcome could have been different in 2014 or after. Opportunity came up and I didn't let it slip away. I may or may not run Badwater 135 again. The race is very costly unless enough sponsors support. Training and preparation required full attention. Family, work and a lot of things were affected. I am extremely grateful to have the support of my family and friends.

Seizing the opportunity to capture "One Shot Dream" takes:

Desire to run Badwater 135 – This race was number one in my bucket list for a long time. It takes a lot of pride and honor to wear the much coveted belt buckle from what is considered the "ultimate race". An invitation to the race wouldn't be complete if I left empty handed. There were lots of pressure but focus remained on the goal at the same time fulfilling daily tasks at home and work. Day, night or even in my sleep, Badwater was in my mind. Some people thought I was out of my mind. I simply replied, "Why not? You'll never know until you try."

Respect the distance - Anything can happen in a very long race. Be patient and stick with the training plan. My mantra was to go through and glide through the desert quietly. Run a smart race. Badwater 135 offers little room for mistakes. The beast is very wily and just waiting for the runner to fall into a trap. Caution, don't wake up the beast.

Extreme training – Dealing with the Badwater means runner must be an extremist. An extremist is a person who resorts to measures above and beyond normal activities. Training innovations were developed in preparation for Badwater.

Assembling the "A Team" – Like any sports team draft day, there were so many talented runners available for selection. Finding the right combination that would blend was a huge challenge. My crew composed of runners of variable speeds and character. As one of my crew member, Jay commented, "Who knew bonding with strangers holed up in a van for a couple of days would be fun, eh? All bonded for a common goal. It was an epic adventure."

Mental toughness – When the going gets tough, the tough gets going. Aside from physical training mental preparation is required at Badwater. Speed can be learned and taught but not mental toughness. This has to come from runner himself / herself.

My Badwater finish was not only a victory for myself but to all dreamers.

As the group Aerosmith sings, "Dream on, dream on, Dream On, dream on. Dream until your dream comes true."

15819773R00098

Made in the USA
San Bernardino, CA
08 October 2014